OUT OF THE
SHADOWS

OUT OF THE
SHADOWS

THE GIFT OF ADOPTION

ANDRÉ A. SCOTT

OUT OF THE SHADOWS
THE GIFT OF ADOPTION

iUniverse books may be ordered through booksellers or by contacting:

iUniverse
1663 Liberty Drive
Bloomington, IN 47403
www.iuniverse.com
844-349-9409

Because of the dynamic nature of the Internet, any web addresses or links contained in this book may have changed since publication and may no longer be valid. The views expressed in this work are solely those of the author and do not necessarily reflect the views of the publisher, and the publisher hereby disclaims any responsibility for them.

Any people depicted in stock imagery provided by Getty Images are models, and such images are being used for illustrative purposes only. Certain stock imagery © Getty Images.

ISBN: 978-1-6632-2371-5 (sc)
ISBN: 978-1-6632-2372-2 (e)

Print information available on the last page.

iUniverse rev. date: 07/12/2021

CONTENTS

DEDICATION

I dedicate this book to my late Grandmother, *Sarah Minnie Badger*, who was a major force, in the way I was raised. She was a strong-willed woman of God, who *'tightened me up'* on many occasions. My Grandmother raised seven children of her own and six foster children. *"Thank You... for the lives your love touched."*

December 26, 1995
1:00pm

Bethesda Full Gospel Church
1365 Main Street
Buffalo, New York

OFFICIATING

Pastor Michael Badger

Sarah M. Badger

1917 — 1995

Until We Meet Again

AUTHOR'S NOTE

UNCENSORED

"When father and mother forsake me,
then the Lord will take me up" (Psalms 27:10) KJV

First, I would like to thank God for my life and for keeping me. If it had not been for the Lord on my side, truly I don't know where I would be.

There are some sensitive issues that will be revealed in this book; my goal is not to embarrass my family and friends, but this book had to be written to help myself and others who have experienced **Adoption** issues in the form of emotional, mental and sexual abuse. The word **Abuse** according to Webster's Dictionary, is *to turn from the proper use; to ill-use; to deceive; to vilify; to violate.* If even one of these definitions fits you then this book is for you.

I thank my lovely wife, *Lisa,* for her support in this endeavor. It took many long hours to put this together. I also thank my children, *Andrew, Stephanie and Tiara;* for they sacrificed their father so that many people could be healed. I would also like to thank my entire family for their support.

YOU ARE NOT ALONE

FOREWORD

Amazing & freeing. This is a story of courage, hope and miracles, especially for the "untouchables". As a physician and psychiatrist, I too believe in miracles. But to be this humble, open and honest about yourself is amazing, a rare gem of healing. But this kind of freedom is contagious and allows others to risk opening the closed doors of their hearts to allow hope, healing and freedom in.

Andre openly exposes the most shameful, painful, shocking, disgraceful and forbidden subjects as if they were just a "matter of fact". The power of slavery to mock, humiliate in hopelessness is being broken. Our hidden crookedness is being exposed and straightened out. Andre writes from the point of view of a healer, therapist and an injector of hope. "Since I got free, so you can you."

People just don't talk about these things, especially men. This "Boldly Honest", even matter of fact style from a male is rare and refreshing.

The "Great Bounce Back": Andre's story is about the power of resurrection & resilience: Knocked down but not out & he keeps getting up and keeps getting stronger! Though killed but keeps getting resurrected. Molested but not on the "down-low", "punked-off" but not a punk, abandoned but not forsaken. Abused but not an abuser.

This "Anointed Power" gives strength in weakness, blessings in dying, life thru death. Left for dead but still living. Truly a wounded healer, a minister to ministers.

Our society is so ready for an honest but powerful path to freedom. We are tired of the phony foolishness of the media. We know the "truth will set you free", but who is willing to tell the truth. Andre's heart of compassion to rescue the most broken & desperate people, like himself, and all of us, is a breath of fresh air in these troubled COVID times.

In a way we are all father-less orphans, since our original father (Adam) abandoned us to a wicked father Satan. Science knows (though not often talked about), that ACE's (Adverse Childhood Events) are at the core of almost all mental and physical diseases, addictions and poverty. As Leif Hetland accurately says the world is an orphanage, a house full of orphans, searching for their real father (Heavenly Father).

Most believe that "Healing the past" from these childhood and generational traumas is impossible. But Bishop TD Jakes is fond of saying: "This is a job for JESUS". He is the same healer: "yesterday, today and forever".

Andre demonstrates this power of the Great Physician to heal the impossible, over & over in his own life. Despite all hell breaking loose.

This is a truly a must read. The secret of hope & healing is revealed.

André has found his calling & giftings, the Keys to set multitudes free. Let this story open the door to your opportunities for healing too.

Dr. Leeland A. Jones, MD
Whole Person Consultant & Advisor
Author of *Becoming Whole: Being the Beloved*

I believe that this book will bring healing to many people. Andre's transparency allows God to heal those places that Satan wants us to keep covered.

The Bible declares in Genesis concerning Adam and Eve that they were naked and not ashamed.

Andre allows God replace his leaves with the truth of God's word.

It is the Great Exchange where God takes his ashes and gives him Beauty, what God did for Andre he wants to do for all of us.

As you read this book and allow God's truth to take off the leaves of shame and cover you with the truth of His glory!

Bishop Michael Badger

PREFACE

I am writing this book for those who have been wounded and bruised because of situations beyond their control, for those who have been taken from one place to another, tossed in despair and without a hope in the world. This is for you... **THERE IS HOPE!**

This book is not only for adults, but for teenagers, and children who have dealt with and/or currently dealing with emotional mental and sexual abuse.

Life seems to have many uncertainties and as we travel through it, we learn many different things. There is a saying *"there is light at the end of the tunnel"* and that is a true statement. The problem, however, is that in the state of mind we are sometimes in; we don't see the end of the tunnel and we don't see the light... we only see the present and it is *darkness*. There is a *Prophet* by the name of *Kim Clement* who has a saying *"You're somewhere in the future and you look much better than you do right now."* Believe this as you read this book.

There is dysfunction in every family and mine was no exception. Only with the help of God, can we overcome this dysfunction, as long as we do not lose *HOPE*.

In preparing to write this book, I had many doubts and fears. For many years, I felt that I needed to write, but because of my fears of failure, shame and bitterness, it seemed impossible. But, here it is, *"the truth, the whole truth and nothing but the truth **so help me God**."* It has taken many years to get to this point, and while I know that it's a process, this book is about from *then to now*. I have come to understand that, *"it ain't over til it's over."* I have adopted this saying into my life, *"it ain't over til God says so."*

INTRODUCTION

The use of the word black instead of African American is not to exclude other men and woman of color.

Adoption has been a difficult process throughout time, and it has caused much controversy. State adoption agencies has had such a time placing children in good homes, many times because of the lack of suitable homes children are forced into; crowded state homes, institutions or put into homes with people who don't care for the children but see it as a means of a supplemental income.

At the time there was a big market for young children/babies. Some people want them because they love children and want to give them a good and safe home. Some wanted these babies because they couldn't have one of their own due to female complications, or the male partner unable to produce viable seed. There are many reasons why.

There is a much smaller number of families who wanted older children, so the courts became overcrowded and under manned. Many children seemed to slip through the cracks and end up with families who didn't care about them, but just wanted a *Pay day*. (These children are hurt and wounded and often forgotten about).

(Jeremiah 1:5a "Before I formed you in the womb I knew you;) spirit filled

God loves us all and before you were born he knew you and his purpose for you.

Before writing this book, I talked with several people who were wounded through the adoption process. This led me to understand that adoption affects *all* people in different ways. The way it has affected my life is the reason why I'm writing this book; it's to show how the choices that people make in life can affect more than themselves.

Adoption can have a very positive outcome, as it has for me, and it also has many tragic outcomes as well. But, it's my process that I want to share with you, so that it brings some hope to those who see no hope. And I hope that through this book, you can see God has a plan for your life just like he had one for mine. David said in *(Psalm 27:10) though my father and mother sake me, the Lord will receive me. NIV.* This is to let you know that He even knows where you have been and even where you're going. My life is an example of what God can do in a submitted life and you will see from birth, God had His hand on my life and has protected me through it all, *because He had a purpose for my life.* I was not a mistake or born at the wrong time, but I was **"born for such a time as this."**

I pray that many lives would be saved, yoke of bondages broken, family patterns broken and prison doors opened and those who are caught in this web of anger, bitterness and deception, believe that you are worthless, and believe you will never amount to anything or that you were born a mistake and no one loves you, I pray that God will touch your heart and bring you to the truth that He created all things, (*Colossians 1:16*) and that includes you! Yes you… God said that you were good and that you are beautifully and wonderfully made.

CHAPTER 1

THE BEGINNING

IT STARTED A LONG TIME ago, about 57 years to be exact. On a cold Buffalo, New York's October night, a moment of intimate lust, my father's seed found an available and willing egg from my mother. This perfect union produced me. You may be asking yourself *"why is he going there?"* I am going there because that was where it all began. That night their lives changed forever and my life began. My parents didn't know that in a month or so, life as they knew it would be changed forever. At such a young age and with no cares in the world, little did they know, that was all about to change. *"Ready or not, here I come!"*

My mother had rheumatic fever as a child and because of this, whenever she got sick it was always necessary that a doctor see her. My grandmother noticed that she had a cold, one that she couldn't seem to shake, so she took her to Dr. Lee. After a checkup, blood test and urine test, she was sent home. At that time, this was the process. Doctors sent patients home and called them later with the test results.

After a few days, grandma got a call from Dr. Lee and was told they needed to come and see him. Once back at Dr. Lee's office, they were informed that she was pregnant. She was confused and told Dr. Lee that it was impossible for her to be pregnant because she had her menstrual period. Dr. Lee advised mom that the urine tests don't lie and that she was indeed pregnant. She felt anxiety and a rush of feelings that she never felt before. Feelings of uncertainty and fear took over her emotions. She finally realized the truth, *"I am pregnant!"* The question was asked, *"Do you want an abortion?"* She replied, *"No, I'm going to keep my baby."* Days later, she was able to catch up with the suspected sperm donor, but when she told him that she was pregnant and the baby was his, he replied, *"I don't believe you."* It was a lot for him to swallow at that time, so she told *'his mother'* that she was pregnant.

A while later, after things settled, she accepted the fact that she was pregnant and *wondered* what to do. The numbness had passed and reality set in. And, because she decided to keep the baby, she had to withstand humiliation by adults and youth alike. You see, Mom was sixteen and pregnant, and in those days, it wasn't fashionable to be pregnant without being married; it was even worse being so young *with child*. Times have surely changed. Today, it seems to be fashionable, as young ladies post pictures on all the social media sites, all the time now. Nevertheless, Mom continued going to school until her pregnancy began to show. In those days, one couldn't attend regular schools while pregnant, so she was sent to *Booth Memorial School* for pregnant students.

Nine months later, the time had come for me to arrive and I was about to make my grand entrance. The doctors and nurses had all arrived; waiting for me to burst on the scene. I have a captive audience, "*PUSH*," the doctor said, "*PUSH!*" Finally, I was born, screaming at the top of my little lungs. "Brrrh, it's cold out here... What's going on?... Who are you?"

As you can see, I was not born under ideal conditions. My parents were young and full of life; just like many of your parents. You may have come into this world like myself or you may have had parents who were married and you were not conceived out of wedlock; however, you came in, does not really matter, but what does matter is how you go out. My parents never married but remained good friends until the day my father (*Dennis*) was laid to rest on, *March 1, 2010.*

Keep in mind, the way a person comes in this world does not determine process or the ending. Our lives are like a book, there is a beginning, middle and an ending; it may read like a horror story or a fairytale. What determines which one is the middle or the filling is determined by you... '*Yes you!*' How you handle conflict, hurts, disappointments, abandonment, shame and bitterness will determine the outcome.

There is a story in the book of 1ˢᵗ Samuel, Chapter 16, that's in the Holy Bible, about a young man by the name of David. The first time we hear about David is after King Saul was rejected by God (Yahweh). The prophet Samuel was sent on assignment by God to go to a man named Jesse's house and anoint the next king of Israel, you know the story. Samuel comes to Jesse's house and invited the chief men of the city to join them in celebration of God's choice for the new king. After sifting through 7 sons of Jesse and the Lord God rejects them for the appointment; and there was not another present, to be considered, Samuel asked *"is there another son?"* Jesse replies, *"there is one more out tending to the sheep,"* and to everyone's surprise, who was present, Samuel requested that David be brought before him. David was brought in and the Lord God tells Samuel, *"this is the one that I choose to be king."* This is important... God says that David is his choice, *not* Prophet Samuel or anyone else, *God chooses.*

This story has a great meaning to it, for which, I will get to, at some point in the future, but I want to point to a fact that most of us never knew about this man name David. Up and until the very moment Samuel anointed David as king, he was the *black sheep,* an *outcast,* a *bastard child* of his mother, whose name was *Nitzevet.* Let me define the word BASTARD according to the standard dictionary:

1. A person born of unmarried parents, an illegitimate child.
2. Slang. A vicious, despicable, or toughly disliked person

According to how most of us read 1st Samuel 16, we may have read and assumed that Jesse forgot about one of his sons, but the truth is that he did not forget about him, *as a son*... because he did not believe he was his son. So, as not to bring great shame to his household, he allowed David to be on the family spread. David was sent to do the work of a servant, not only that, but he was sent out to the fields alone to be killed by wild animals. Jesse and his seven other sons were hoping that David would be devoured by the beast of the field; thereby relieving Jesse of dishonor and not killing him with his own hands.

Nitzevet was found to be pregnant and Jesse was furious but because of the culture of the time and Jesse's prominent standing in the community, he did not destroy the man child. According to history, Jesse had put Nitzevet away because he felt that he was illegally married to her according to the *Law of Torah* regarding marriage of an Israelite to a Moabite. Jesse had no relations with her for many years, *(then she was found to be pregnant)*, you can read about this in *'The Bold Voice of Silence by Chana Weisberg.'*

I want us to see that David's life started out quite bad, but in the end, God chose him to be the greatest king that Israel ever had.

So, when David writes in Psalms 27:10, ***"When father and mother forsake me the Lord will take me up,"*** he is reflecting on his life and how he felt during 28 years of hell inside and outside his father's house. -also read Psalms 69 for more clarity on David's troubles. He seemed to be forsaken by all, BUT GOD never forsook him. And Father God, will never forsake you nor abandon you either, no matter what you are facing or going through today. *David was adopted by God... David was chosen by God*!

If you have been rejected by your father or your family, God the Father, wants you to know that He loves you with an everlasting love that can never fail. He wants you to believe this and to accept this as the truth. *Let this truth set you free today*!

NOTES

HOW DO YOU FEEL ABOUT THIS STORY

_____

_____

_____

_____

_____

_____

_____

_____

_____

_____

_____

_____

_____

_____

_____

_____

_____

_____

_____

_____

_____

_____

_____

_____

CHAPTER 2

PIZZA PIZZA PIZZA

TIMON STREET ALSO STANDS OUT in my memory. I see it as if it was yesterday. I was 4 years of age at the time. The house was green with yellow trim; a two-story house. We lived in the upstairs apartment with my family.

One hot summer day, my siblings and I were in the house playing. We ran around and around the apartment, until I hit the ironing board and the iron fell on my brother's hand and burned him very badly, (*he carries the scar til this day*). Mom ran in after hearing the shouts and screaming from my brother and sister, she then put a cold rag on his hand and took him to the hospital where he received treatment and was thereafter released. When my brother returned home that night, he was very angry at me and Mom was quite upset also. I was sent to my room to wait for whom I believed was my stepfather to come home. And, when he arrived later that evening, I was punished and sent to my room. Dinner that night was pizza and my stepfather told me that I was *not* to eat dinner, and he sent me back to my room hungry. I remember the ceiling patterns in my room and how my room was off the kitchen. After the family ate dinner that night, they went outside, but left me hungry. So, I got up and snuck into the kitchen, to see if I could gather up what was left, and found that there was nothing there, *only* the pizza box, in the garbage can. I opened the box just to smell what I had missed and to my surprise, there was a discarded pizza crust in the box, *so the garbage became my dinner.*

I really didn't know how much that had affected me, until I was much older. I like the crust of the pizza just as much as I like the cheese and pepperonis! And, not only did it affect me that way, but I felt that I was not provided for and was left to eat from the trash. I was left to fend for myself.

All my life, I have felt that I had to do it on my own. God had been telling me that He was there for me, and that He would take care of me, but it took me until now to realize that He really was *and is* there for me.

I also felt, all my life, that everything was my fault; that I should be punished, but that was a lie from the enemy too. It was not my fault that I was sent to my room, without dinner and it wasn't proper punishment for a young child.

Christmas time was a wonderful time of the year. One particular Christmas Eve, my family and I were all together and the snow was falling. It was so beautiful outside. We had a tree decorated so nice, but there were no gifts under it. That was okay for us because the tree was so pretty. We asked Mom, '*where were the gifts?*' She told us that Santa Clause would be bringing the toys that night. We believed her just as any child would. *We believed that Santa was on his way, bringing a toy to every boy and every girl*, who had been good all that year.

That night while we were sleeping; I heard a noise that awakened me. I got up from my bed and peeked out from my room. It was a wonderful sight... I saw my stepfather bringing in toys putting them under the tree. From that moment on, I knew that there wasn't a *real* Santa, who brought toys to children, *it was just our parents.*

Our parents are not perfect and Father God knows this. Many children have been subjected to bad parenting and oftentimes our parents learned bad habits from their parents. We must do better and we can. I know that God wants us all to know the truth; that He loves us and He will always be there even when our parents mess up.

NOTES

HOW DO YOU FEEL ABOUT THIS STORY

_____

_____

_____

_____

_____

_____

_____

_____

_____

_____

_____

_____

_____

_____

_____

_____

_____

_____

_____

_____

_____

_____

_____

_____

_____

_____

CHAPTER 3

LEFT BEHIND

I REMEMBER STAYING WITH MY Aunt Jackie for a while, this one time. I talked to her regarding the time when I believed to be about 4 years old, I was at her home and I went out onto the top porch area. I remember climbing over the railing and my younger brother and sister followed. By the way, I didn't tell you that I had a younger brother and sister, did I? Well, we will get to them later. Anyway, Aunt Jackie happened to look outside and saw us out on the ledge. She ran and pulled us off of the ledge and unbeknown to me others were standing below looking up with great concerns for our safety, boy, did she lay into me for that grandstand.

I told my Aunt that I remembered my Uncle Herbert having a W.C. Fields shot pourer; that's when you put a coin in its back, the shot pourer would tip over and pour out liquor into a shot glass. I played with that shot pourer until I broke it. I got a spanking for that, too; then there was another item on the table that captured my interest and it looked like a monk. (You know one of those men who would go into the mountains, away from civilization and take an oath of silence and sexual abstinence. They also shaved their heads and wore brown robes with the ropes tied around their waists, you know it looked like the Friar Tuck from the Robin Hood movie), Anyway, when you pushed his head down, something very amazing would happen. If you have ever seen one of these, then you know what I'm talking about when I say 'by pushing the head down.' The robe would part at the bottom and '*you know what*' would appear. Boy, did I get a kick out of that. That was someone's perverted view of humor. Oftentimes, children at an early age, are exposed to things that they shouldn't be exposed to. I, even described these things to my Aunt; she laughed and wondered how I remembered those things… I told her, "*I just do.*"

Children remember more than what we think; even as far back as in the womb. Everything that we feel, hear and taste has an effect on

9

us. No matter who you are or where you come from. God created man more complex than we can even imagine.

I was told by family members that Aunt Jackie took me in, after my Mom left us with family… saying that *she would be back to get me*, but never returned. I was too young, at the time, to understand the impact that this abandonment would create in my life.

"Can a woman forget her nursing child, and not have compassion on the son of her womb? Surely, they may forget, yet will I not forget you. see, I have inscribed you the palms of my hands; your walls are continually before me." Isaiah 49:15-16 NKJV

The Father will never forsake you!

NOTES

HOW DO YOU FEEL ABOUT THIS STORY

_____

_____

_____

_____

_____

_____

_____

_____

_____

_____

_____

_____

_____

_____

_____

_____

_____

_____

_____

_____

_____

_____

Say this prayer:

Lord, I ask you to wash and cleanse my eye gates and my heart of any seeds of perversion that was planted in my soul as a child. I ask that every spoken words of defilement be removed and set on fire by the holy Spirit. This I ask in the name of Jesus.

CHAPTER 4

THE FIRST AND THE LAST

ONE DAY, AT MY GRANDFATHER'S house, on Humboldt Parkway in Buffalo, *man*, this seemed to be a great time in my life… I spent with him. I remember at that time, they were putting in the expressway (*commonly called Route 33*), which runs east and west. Before the local government began their expressway plans, this place was a bountifully beautiful horse and buggy park with lots of grass and benches. Many wealthy people lived on both sides; though many of the *Whites* who owned the properties began to sell out to the unknowing and unsuspecting *Blacks*, and they moved to the *Suburbs*. Not long after the town board announced that for the betterment of the *City of Buffalo*, they were going to run a road from Downtown to Genesee street which just happens to be in the what?! You got that right *Suburbs*. This literally destroyed the area; which was once beautiful, now had become noisy and polluted. Many of the African Americans who bought those homes, could no longer get the value, for which they had paid for them.

One day, as we were sitting at the dining room table, my grandfather told us to come into the front room. He sat us down and wanted to talk to us. I was not sure what he wanted to talk about; but I knew that it seemed to be important to him, *so I listened.* He then took some beer, (*I can still remember the brand name… It was a tall can of Colt 45. It was a white can with red writing on it and with a red horse*). Anyway, he took the can and told all of us to drink some. Oh, what an awful taste that was, even as I am writing, I can still taste it. Many questions ran through my mind, at that time; but after we drank the beer, my grandfather told us that he made us taste it because he didn't want us to turn out like him. You see, my grandfather had a very serious addiction to alcohol. *Again, my family was not perfect.*

Many times, we judge our parents or grandparents, *by what they have done,* but now I look at what he did, not with judgment but with a sense of *thank you Lord.* You may be asking, '*what in the world is he talking about?'* I thank the Lord, not for the drink of beer, but for my grandfather seeing himself and what he had become and not wanting it to be passed on to us. I know and you know that *that* was not the proper way to stop us from drinking. And he did subject us to alcohol at a young age. At the time, he did all that he knew how to do or understood *to do.* That is why I say, *thank you Lord.* Today, I can say beer has never touched my lips again since that day and I am drug and alcohol free.

Matthew 7:1-3 KJV

Judge not, that ye be not judged. For with what judgement ye judge, ye shall be judged: and with what measure ye mete, it shall be measured to you again.

Be careful how you judge other people, for by the same harsh judgement you bring towards them, you will receive the same measure. Don't be quick to judge but consider they own self.

NOTES

HOW DO YOU FEEL ABOUT THIS STORY

_____

_____

_____

_____

_____

_____

_____

_____

_____

_____

_____

_____

_____

_____

_____

_____

_____

_____

_____

_____

_____

_____

_____

CHAPTER 5

AN ACT OF GOD

My siblings and I became *"Wards of the State."* We were not sent to a correctional facility, but became foster children (to some, they are both the same). *John and LaVera Scott* already had two children and were thinking about foster children; just by chance, they heard about someone who had three children that needed a family. Let me tell you how this all came about.

My mother got married to a man who was in the Navy. He was not only in the Navy, but was a pilot and traveled quite a bit. Once again, my mom took ill and her heart was so weak that her doctor advised her to let someone keep the children for a while, because of the stress that she was under; she could have had a heart attack. So, my aunt decided to take care of us. When I talked with my aunt on the telephone, she told me that when mom left; my aunt was under the impression that our mother would be coming back to get us... *but she never did.* After about six months, when she did not return, my aunt received a call from Social Services and later, a visit regarding the three children that she was keeping. She was told that something had to be done. We had to be placed in a *foster home.* My aunt told them that we were *'already at home,'* but the system felt that my uncle was too old and unable to take care of three children. You see, my uncle was missing his left arm and that disqualified him and my aunt as suitable parents, *according to the system.* A representative from Social Services came out to visit us and as she was leaving, my aunt remembered John and LaVera Scott, who mentioned that they wanted to take care of foster children. She called the representative back and told her of *the Scott's.* The social worker then gave the Scott's a call; but told them that they could not have all three of us. *We would have to be separated.* That was not acceptable to the Scott's! Although, at that time they already had two children of their own; they felt that it was *out of the question* to split us up. So, LaVera had to meet with the caseworker about this and she told the caseworker that if she couldn't have all three of us, she wouldn't take any of us. She was not going to be a part of separating us. Further, she told the caseworker that we had been through enough. The caseworker talked with her boss and as she did; *God moved on our behalf.* They agreed to allow the Scott family to take *all three of us.* The Scott's were told that we could not sleep in the same bed, so they went out and bought bunk beds for us to sleep on.

You must understand what took place. At that time, in the 1960's, people wanted children and there were not a lot of babies available in the system. Because of our ages, we were prime for those who wanted children. *Social Services* were a tough bunch to work with, too. If you have ever dealt with them, you would know what (mom) had to go through to get the department to agree with her taking all three of us. She had to *beg* them not to separate us and not cause any more trauma to our lives. The social worker felt that it would be impossible for them to have all three of us and that it would take an act of God. Well, I know God showed up because we then came to live with the Scott family.

You may be facing an impossible situation at this very moment and see no way out (Philippians 4:13) I can do all things through Christ whose strength is in me, that means that I have the strength of God flowing through my veins and there is nothing I cannot do through Christ, *that's right*, if you try it alone you can expect possible failure. But, if you choose to make Christ your partner then you cannot fail... because He cannot fail. Glory to God, *John and LaVera* understood this and stood on God's word and trusted Him and *Him alone did they trust.*

> *Romans 8:28, "And we know that all things work together for the good to them that love God, to them that are called according His purpose."*

17

NOTES

HOW DO YOU FEEL ABOUT THIS STORY

_____

_____

_____

_____

_____

_____

_____

_____

_____

_____

_____

_____

_____

_____

_____

_____

_____

_____

_____

_____

_____

_____

_____

_____

_____

CHAPTER 6

THE ADOPTION

THE SCOTT'S TOOK GOOD CARE of us. It came time for them to make a decision in their family by taking our relationship to another level; that is to adopt the three of us into their family. By having their own children, there was a lot for them to consider. We had been with them for about 8 years at that point. I knew that I was not the best child, that I could have been, since I was angry and bitter most of the time and sometimes I would think about my parents and wonder what was wrong with me or why did they just throw me away; so, I wouldn't have blamed the Scott's, if they had not wanted to keep us, with *my* bad attitude.

Yet, the day had come, however, when mom came to us and said that she had something to ask us. We were all present and accounted for. Mom and Dad asked, '*how would we feel if they were to adopt us?*' We were not sure what *adoption* meant, so I asked them, I thought all along that we belonged to them, but mom explained that as a foster child, we still really belonged to the State Service Department and at any time, they could come and take us away and place us in a new home with different people. We could even be separated. *Afterwards, I understood very clearly what she meant by adoption.* She asked us again whether we wanted to be a permanent part of their family and we all said "*yes.*" Then she asked her natural children if they wanted us as brothers and sisters. They all said, "*yes*" too. Mom told us that the reason they waited so long to adopt us was so that we would be at the age to make the choice on our own based on the time we had spent in their family.

On October 3, 1978, sometime in the morning, we all went down to the Federal Courthouse. We went into a room where mom and dad were talking to some people as we sat down and waited for them to finish. We were all dressed up and looked very nice. After a stretch of time, dad and mom came over and talked to us and told us to wait a little longer. Mom brought some papers over to us and said that at this time, to be adopted meant that we could change our last name, then she asked if there were any other changes, we might want to make; if so… now was the time to make them. This was great for me, because I didn't like my name, (my name was Andrey Pernell Beecher). I was not happy with that name and I wanted to disassociate myself from any part of that name, just like my biological parents abandoned me and rejected me… I rejected my name. One reason for my dislike of my name, was when I started school, the teacher would always pronounce my name Audrey Beecher and I would get so mad and say "It's Andrey." That's not all; the children would call me "peery." They would tease me and I would cry. They would also call me "Beech Nut Gum" because of my last name. Children can be so cruel. Anyway, mom gave us the forms to fill out for the name changes. I changed my name from Andrey Pernell Beecher to Andre' Anthone Scott. My younger sister and brother retained Beecher Scott to the end of their name.

A large man finally came over and asked us to go with him. We went into another room and stood up before a man in a robe who looked like a penguin. He looked over our papers and spoke to dad and mom. Thereafter, he addressed us and asked if we understood what was taking place, we said "yes." I was twelve years old and understood pretty well what was taking place in the natural realm that is, but not in the spiritual. The judge signed our papers and stamped some things, then he congratulated us and said now we were really a part of the Scott family. He told us that he would be checking in on us from time to time. But, I don't remember ever seeing him from that day forward.

On that day, we all hugged and kissed and cried.

I was so angry at my biological parents that I refused to retain any part of the name they gave me at birth, I wanted total distance and disconnected myself from them, so as to cut them off from my life completely. This was the time to make a statement against them for abandoning me… for rejecting me as a son. The pain and thoughts of that moment was confusing. I had emotions of joy, then at the same time emotions of anger and hatred towards my biological parents. I had pinned up rage, one might say, "unchecked and dangerous," and if not dealt with appropriately could prove detrimental to not only myself but others.

Family Court of The State of New York
COUNTY OF ERIE

CERTIFICATE OF ADOPTION

STATE OF NEW YORK } ss.:
COUNTY OF ERIE

I, Frank J. Boccio, Clerk of the Family Court of the said County, do hereby certify that I have inspected the records of this Court in the matter of Adoptions and find that:

AN ORDER OF ADOPTION was signed on the 3rd day of October, 1978, by HON. EDWARD V. MAZUR, Judge of the Family Court of the County of Erie, granting the petition of John Howard Scott and LaVera Nannette Scott his wife, then residing at 228 Strauss Street, Buffalo, N.Y. for the adoption of a minor child now known and called by the name of Andre Anthone Scott who was born at Buffalo, New York on the 4th day of February, 1964, and directing that the child shall henceforth be regarded and treated in all respects as the child of said petitioners.

IN TESTIMONY WHEREOF, I have hereunto set my hand and affixed the seal of the Family Court of the County of Erie, this 3rd day of October in the year of our Lord, one thousand nine hundred Seventy-eight.

Frank J. Boccio

Clerk of the Family Court of the County of Erie

21

NOTES

HOW DO YOU FEEL ABOUT THIS STORY

_____

_____

_____

_____

_____

_____

_____

_____

_____

_____

_____

_____

_____

_____

_____

_____

_____

_____

_____

_____

_____

_____

_____

_____

CHAPTER 7

THE DAY I DIED

ONE DAY OUR PARENTS LEFT us home alone, in the care of my older siblings, there were other cousins and family members over that day, as well. This day was ordinary, just like any other day; but with one exception, on this day... *my life took a turn.*

As we were playing, for some very sick reason, one of the older children forced myself and another boy to commit an oral sexual act on each other. With tears in our eyes, we were afraid and ashamed of committing this perverted act on each other. *I was sick all over* and I was only about nine years old, so I didn't understand what was happening to me. While this was going on, it was as if time stood still and I felt as though I was dead. *I died that day*! I don't remember hearing anything, except my soul crying out for help. Here I was, a child innocent, without a care in the world and in one single tick tock of the clock, my life took a turn forever. My purity and innocence stolen by a thief. I can remember it as if it happened yesterday. I'm not describing this to make you uncomfortable; only to tell my story and how each event affected my life for *many years*, and how this similar situation has affected your life also. It had an effect on me, until I was well into my forties.

When *the act* was over, we were told not to say anything, to any one because we were in on it too; this was *a lie mixed with the truth*. The real truth was and *still is* that I was forced into doing something out of fear and confusion. I did not ask for this to happen to me; *but it was done to me*. That does not make me guilty of any wrongdoing. This is how predators and wicked men control and keep their victims silent. They use fear, guilt and shame to control their prey and they lie to them; to keep them in bondage.

Sadly, there were other family members there that day, but no one spoke a word or came to my rescue. I mentioned it to no one. I have kept this secret until now. I believed it was my fault that I allowed myself to be put into this situation. I became very rebellious after this; full of anger and rage, **any trust I had was now dead along with the person that died in me**. The other child involved; *he and I never spoke of it again*.

There is a shame and embarrassment that comes with *abuse* and it stuck with me for most of my life. You want to forget it, hide it away in the deep recesses of your mind, to be lost forever, but that doesn't work. I know! The memory rings on and on sounding like a huge bell ringing in the night. There are times when I would seem to forget, but then there is something that triggers it. It may be a simple word or something I saw on the news or even a smell. *Yes, a smell*! God gave man a powerful sense of smell and some traumas come with a smell and certain smells can trigger a negative or positive memory or emotion that causes a total recall; just as if it was happening all over again. People would look at me from the outside and think things were okay, that I had it all together, because I could put on a good front, but all I really was doing was wearing a **mask.** Yes, we are a very creative people. We all wear mask every day *and*, in every situation, but what others did not see… was the truth; *I was living in my own hell*.

You just can't tuck abuse away and forget about it. It will affect your whole life and your only freedom is in forgiveness through Jesus Christ. **You won't find it in the bottom of a Hennessey bottle or drugs or sex; these don't remove the pain, it only numbs you for a while and adds a new twist to the problem. It's like adding gasoline to a house fire in attempts to put it out.**

I had the opportunity, many years later, in my forties, to sit with and confront the male who facilitated the sexual act between myself and the other child. He spoke with me and with tears in his eyes, asked for my forgiveness. God told me to go see him… *this was not easy*, but I obeyed the voice of the Lord. *Yes, to answer your question, God does speak to me*! He also speaks to you, in a still small voice. The question is, will you listen and obey. The Lord had prepared my heart before I met with him at his home. Before I could say anything to him… he said, "I know what you are here for." **God will prepare you for what you have to deal with… if you let him**.

We were on the fourth day of a fast at our church and the Lord was dealing with us on forgiveness. A word came forth… God was breaking down the walls of *un*-forgiveness that we might be free from the yoke of sin and bondages through *un*-forgiveness. God allowed me to revisit that day of the abuse. He asked me, *will I give it up.* By asking, *"loveth thou these more than me?"(John 12:15) KJV*

You see, Jesus asked Peter after He had allowed them to catch a multitude of fish that almost turned over their boats, (*I was dumb founded and then it hit me*), the question was *do I love my anger and bitterness more than I love the Lord, will I be obedient…* that night, I stood up before the church and said what God spoke about bondage and I released the person who hurt and abused me. You see, the Lord prepared me because I chose to let it go. If I chose not to forgive him it could have wreaked havoc on me and I might have done him physical harm or worse *by my hands.* **Many people say they can handle it, but truthfully, it's handling you. There was a root of bitterness in my heart and for something to have a root, it first must begin with a seed and if there is a seed, there will be a tree, and if there is a tree, then there will be fruit and that fruit can be bitter or sweet, it's up to you.** My fruit was bitter and bitterness leads to anger and anger makes you foolish and anger will cause you do things outside of your character. Did you know that the word *hate* is translated as murder *"pause"* and *"think."* You have to destroy the fruit and the root through forgiveness." *"Looking carefully lest there be any man that falls short of the grace of God; lest any root of bitterness springing up trouble you, and thereby the many be defiled." (Heb. 12:15)* ASV *God* is saying clearly, if bitterness is allowed to fester in you, then it has the power or ability to harm others, even those whom you love. *Hurt people hurt people.*

I know there are some of you out there who had similar experiences and have not chosen to forgive or even knew that you should, forgiveness is a choice. It's a choice of your will and God commands us to forgive our brothers. The disciples asked Jesus *"how many times must we forgive our brother and Jesus said to forgive him seventy times seven." (Matt. 18:22).* It is a proven scientific fact that any one harboring bitterness and anger; that it eats away at them and cause health problems, such as cancer; this eats away at the body, much like how bitterness eats away at your soul and will infect others also. Jesus wants you to forgive so that he can heal you and make you whole. *"And when you stand praying, forgive, if you have ought against any: that your Father which also is in heaven may forgive you your trespasses." (Mark 11:25) KJV*

I know you may say, it was wrong, what they've done, I have a right to be angry and bitter. You are right, you can get angry, but the problem is when you do not release it unto the Father, it *becomes* sin. I know that you are going to say that Jesus got angry and overturned the tables in the house of God, ***"And made a scourge of small cords, he drove them all out of the temple, and the sheep, and the oxen: and poured out the changers' money, and overthrew the table; (Jn. 2:15) KJV*** Jesus was angry because the changers were selling these items to the people using weighted scales, they were cheating the people coming to the temple of their God. *"and he had a right to do so, but the difference here is that he sinned not; also, that this was righteous indignation, the apostle Paul says it this way,* ***"be angry but sin not." (Eph.4:26) KJV "We must abandon our right to be right"*** what does that mean? Well, sometimes in this life, we have to make tough decisions; when to know *when your right* leads you to be wrong. You are right, you have the right to be angry about being violated, but what makes your right wrong is your improper response to what was done or not done, instead of getting bitter and allowing hatred to fester within; you have to **"Bless those who curse you, pray for those who hurt you" (Luke 6:28)**. Wow that's crazy… *is it not?* To bless the one who molested me and pray for those who hurt me? **Yes, this is what the word tells us. If we do it Gods way, we will reap the God kind of results**. What results are you getting now?

King David for 28 years was accused of stealing from the town's people, he was accused of all kinds of things of which he was innocent, but the Lord God vindicated him from all the shame, embarrassments and ridicule, as he was crowned King. God wants to do the same for you; he wants to but a crown of glory on you.

If anyone had the right not to forgive, it would had been Jesus Christ. He was accused of things he had not done. He was lied upon, beaten and spit upon. He knew no sin, yet, he chose to become sin and put on this sinful flesh that he may redeem us back to the Father, that we may live full prosperous, purposeful and productive lives. He who had no sin put on sin and shame that we my live. Christ after all said, *"Father forgive them for they know not what they do." (Luke 23:34) KJV. He did it for you!*

My Brother's Keeper / When good people do nothing

Looking at the state of the world today, let me just localize it to America. I see people filming on their camera's and now on their cell phones, it's interesting that we want to get noticed on Facebook, tic tok, Instagram, Twitter and many other forms of media communication by showing something *bad* happening. What's not so funny is that while we are standing there filming or just even standing around watching these things take place, we do not attempt to stop it but we get pleasure out of watching it. Do you know how many people would be alive today if only someone would have intervened? **George Floyd**, a young black man murdered by a police officer, as the officer putting his knee on this man's neck, thereby causing asphyxiation. The officers on scene watched and did nothing as George Floyd cried out for his breath *and* life. If just one of them would have said something, George Floyd would be alive today.

As I look back at when I was nine years of age and was forced to commit a heinous sexual act, I realized that there was many family members there in the house, at that time and many if not all of them stood by and watched this happen to me, some turned their backs and did not want to see it, yet they did not stop it; some watched with amazement but they did nothing to prevent it, and others just stood and enjoyed it.

"Am I My Brother's Keeper," (Geneses 4:9) KJV, this quote we find in the bible where there were twin brothers Cain and Abel, the first born of Adam and Eve. Cain kills his twin brother Abel after they both bring their gifts to God and laid them before Him. God rejects Cain's offering and accepts Abel's. Abel becomes angry with God and his brother; he lures his brother away from the house and family and kills Abel in the field. When God comes to Cain and asked him, *"Where is thy brother?"* Cain responded by saying, I do not know... *"Am I my brother's keeper?"*

Many people are asking the same question today as Cain asked God, *"Am I my brother's keeper?"* What does this have to do with you and I...

I am glad you asked; when good people stand by and do nothing, we are not a part of the solution, but a part of the problem. When you stand by and say nothing and do nothing, you are as guilty as the one who performs the act *against the other*. We cannot wash our hands as Pilate did when Jesus was brought to him by the chief priest, who had the authority to free Jesus. Pilot said, '*I wash my hands of this matter,*' in other words, '*I know it's wrong but I will not take responsibility for what you chose to do.*' That was and is the cowardly way out.

Those who were present when I was abused that day, for their own reasoning they did nothing and for many years, I ate with them… I slept in the same house with them… I played with them… I even went over to their houses; but I never trusted them again. The very ones who had the responsibility to watch over me… failed me. It was not for many years later during the time the Lord was dealing with me about forgiveness, that I was able to completely forgive them all. I never confronted them about it and I don't have to have a face to face; but with the Lord's help, I was able to release myself from bondage to my past and release them from the account and debt, *I believed they owed me*. Let me say this, forgiveness is not for the other person, forgiveness is for you. Get free today… forgive your neighbor forgive your family and your friend – it doeth good like a medicine. You cannot do it in your own strength. You need the strength of the Lord; lean and trust Him. **"God is our refuge and strength, an ever-present help in trouble." (Psalms 46:1-3).** Just trust Him!

NOTES

HOW DO YOU FEEL ABOUT THIS STORY

_____

_____

_____

_____

_____

_____

_____

_____

_____

_____

_____

_____

_____

_____

_____

_____

_____

_____

_____

_____

_____

_____

_____

_____

_____

CHAPTER 8

SURPRIZE SURPRIZE SURPRIZE

ONE YEAR WHEN MY SISTER was in the fourth grade, my sister's teacher was reading the list of names for the class. She wanted to make sure that everyone who was supposed to be in that class was present. She also wanted to make sure that those who weren't supposed to be there would be sent to where they belonged. You know, as well as I do, that there is always some sort of mix up. This particular day… was no different. The teacher called my sister's name and then called the name of another student, *Davon Beecher*. The teacher realized that there were two Beecher's in that class and thought there was some mistake, (as they didn't allow brothers and sisters to be in the same classroom). They both informed the teacher that they were not related; my sister came home and told us about what had taken place in her class.

Beecher was not a common name back then and we didn't know what *common* was; but we could see that my mother was concerned about this. My sister returned to school and Davon was there again, they talked and asked each other who their parents were. My sister told mom and dad who the father of this boy was, at that time, my siblings and I didn't know our natural father's name. One month or so after that, I noticed this handsome gentleman walking past our house on Strauss Street. I would see him many times during the week; he would just look at us and keep on moving. One day, I asked mom about our natural parents. I had become very curious and I needed to know. So, mom told us our father and mother's names; that's when something clicked in me and I asked, *if we could go and see them*. She told us that because of the stipulations of the adoption, we were unable to see them or have any contact with them, *in any way*. This I did not understand, so I got angry. I felt that they just didn't want us to see our natural parents. The need in me to meet them became stronger than ever. A year or so after that, I followed the boy we called *Beecher*. I followed him to a house right around the corner from the school. I didn't approach him, but I watched him. I did this for a couple of days until one day, I saw a man come out with a little baby. Then, about one week later, I saw him walk pass the house, while we were playing. I am not sure how the conversation started, but once it did and I found out that he was my biological father. I had so many questions that I could not even ask *then*. I guess it shocked me, to hear him say that he was my father. I thought it would make me feel better to see him and to get to know who he was, *but it didn't*. It only made me angrier and more confused.

In every man and every woman there is a need to know where we come from but because of bitterness and woundedness we often attempt to block out those feelings; we even bury them as if to try to get rid of them. I found out that burying these things alive only covers them up for a while, sooner or later it's going to re-surface and you'll be back at the same place again. We must face our issues and problems; not try to run or hide from them… *but face them*.

It dawned on me many years later that my biological father had been checking on me for years, he would walk past our home several times a week and say hello. I just thought that he was a nice man who lived in the neighborhood, come to find out it was him. He would pass by and did not reveal his true identity until that one day. I cursed his name, I judged him wrongly out of my own hurts and abandonment issues. It felt good to know that he really cared.

NOTES

HOW DO YOU FEEL ABOUT THIS STORY

_____

_____

_____

_____

_____

_____

_____

_____

_____

_____

_____

_____

_____

_____

_____

_____

_____

_____

_____

_____

_____

_____

CHAPTER 9

LOVE HURTS

AT TWELVE YEARS OLD, AS I stated earlier, I was not the best child. I seemed to be in trouble *every day*. My last name should have been "*trouble.*" I was on punishment most of the summer and was always into something. My younger brother and I were very competitive, we seemed to be always fighting about something or another, either I was putting on his clothing or vice-versa, something was always going on. One day, we started fighting and I don't remember why, I *could always handle him, though*, but on this particular day, my older brother, jumped in and held me down on the floor and coaxed my younger brother to beat me with an empty Clorox bottle. To say the least, I was very angry with my older brother.

We had five dogs and my favorite one was *Bo*, he was a big German shepherd and everyone other than family was afraid of him; many times, during the summer when I was on punishment, I would let Bo out of the gate when no one was looking, then I would yell, "the dog was loose." Mom would always tell us to get him. I would be gone for hours playing with my friends and then return home, I don't think mom ever caught on, if she did, she never spoke of it.

Dad was working a lot. He would come home from working at Nabisco and he'd leave to sell his products. He sold Watkins products. Dad would barely be at home, but when he was, he took care of business. I was in trouble a lot and when mom would get tired of yelling at me, she would tell me to wait until my father got home. Oftentimes, I would be in the bed when he came home, so I thought I had gotten away. *Oh, how wrong I was!* Sometimes, on the weekends, Dad would be off from his job at the plant; he'd call me into the room and talk to me about what my mother told him, afterwards he would take off his belt and tear my tail up, but when the belt had little effect on me, I graduated to the *extension cord*, trust me *that would cure your problems.*

One day, dad sat me down on the bed after he gave me a *good lickin'.*

He talked to me and said that he did this because he loved me and that it hurt him more than it hurt me, imagine that… that the *lickin'* hurt him more than it hurt me; *I thought that was crazy*! I asked myself, "*Isn't there a better way to show me that you love me?*" I realize today, that Dad showed me the love of a father; if he had just let me go without correction, then the bible says… *he hates me.* God says, "**He chasten them that he loves**," *(Hebrew 12:6).*

Many of the friends that I grew up with did things wrong but seemed never to get in trouble. I, on the other hand, got in trouble every time. I would say how I wish I had parents like them; they did not care, but I really did not know what I was saying. Not too long ago, I saw a young man who was one of those children who never got into trouble, he looked rough and old; life really did a job on him. This young man said to me, that he wishes he could have grown up in my family and had parents who was there and cared about him enough to correct him; then he would not have gotten caught up in drugs and gone to prison. *Children need correction*, if it is not given then the child will run amuck… without restraints, and that's trouble… big trouble. So, I thank my dad for loving me enough to give correction. It helped make me who I am today. We all need *appropriate* discipline and correction at some point, in and throughout our lives, and I stress the point of "*appropriate.*"

> **"No discipline is enjoyable while it is happening–it's painful! But afterwards there will be a peaceful harvest of right living for those who are trained in this way." (Hebrews 12:11), NLT**

NOTES

HOW DO YOU FEEL ABOUT THIS STORY

CHAPTER 10

BETRAYAL

Family Court of The State of New York

COUNTY OF ERIE

CERTIFICATE OF ADOPTION

STATE OF NEW YORK } ss.:
COUNTY OF ERIE }

I, Frank J. Boccio, Clerk of the Family Court of the said County, do hereby certify that I have inspected the records of this Court in the matter of Adoptions and find that:

AN ORDER OF ADOPTION was signed on the _3rd_ day of _October_, 19_78_, by HON. _EDWARD V. MAZUR_, Judge of the Family Court of the County of Erie, granting the petition of _John Howard Scott_ and _LaVera Nannette Scott_ his wife, then residing at _228 Strauss Street, Buffalo, N.Y._ for the adoption of a minor child now known and called by the name of _Andre Anthone Scott_ who was born at _Buffalo, New York_ on the _4th_ day of _February_, 19_64_, and directing that the child shall henceforth be regarded and treated in all respects as the child of said petitioners.

IN TESTIMONY WHEREOF, I have hereunto set my hand and affixed the seal of the Family Court of the County of Erie, this _3rd_ day of _October_ in the year of our Lord, one thousand nine hundred _seventy – eight_

Frank J. Boccio
Clerk of the Family Court of the County of Erie

MANY YEARS LATER, I FOUND out that my birth mother had twin girls by her husband, *this grieved me.* I was confused and the more I thought about it, anger swelled up within me. Re-occurring thoughts like *'I wasn't good enough for her so she gave me up and left me with someone else, then had some other children,'* plagued my mind. This was a bad time for me, because not only was I dealing with *abandonment*, now added to that issue was *rejection. 'How could she do this?'*

As a child, I was not told of my mother's circumstances and if I was, I'm not sure if it would have made a difference. Children do not have the mental compacity to rationalize or comprehend these issues; they only go on what they feel and *what they feel is very real*. I became bitter and hateful.

For years, I wondered what they were like *and* what they looked like, all the while angry and jealous that they were even born and living somewhere with my mother.

When we allow bitterness into our heart, it *blocks out* all rational and reasoning. It will take the hand of God to come and root out the infected area and cleanse it with His blood and love. Because of our ignorance, oftentimes we create our own point of view and that in itself *becomes a problem*. Ignorance does not mean one is dumb or stupid, it just means not knowing. In my case not knowing the truth left me to my own understanding. When left to our own understanding, we then only see from the point of our *hurt and pain*.

Let me break it down for you… We act from our experiences; if our experiences are bad, then we respond from that place. So, I was hurt by being abandoned and now there are two others with my mother after she gave me up. Out of that place, I judged my mother and cut her off from my life.

It was 40 plus years later, before I found out some truths and was humbled to repent and ask forgiveness from my mother and my father, in return they asked me to forgive them also for their actions and I was able to forgive them and more importantly, I choose to forgive. Forgiveness is a choice.

> *"For if you forgive men their trespasses, your heavenly Father will also forgive you. But if you don't forgive men their trespasses, neither will your Father forgive your trespasses." (Matthew 6:14-15)*

NOTES

HOW DO YOU FEEL ABOUT THIS STORY

CHAPTER 11

INDECENT EXPOSURE

ONE DAY, I CAME HOME from playing basketball, at that time, all I did during the summer months, from sun up to sun down, was play basketball. You would find me at Dr. Martin Luther King, Jr. Park (*Humboldt Park*), and playing ball. On this particular day, I came home early and went upstairs where my brothers and I rooms were; I had to use the bathroom but it was being occupied by one of my older sister's friends. I spoke through the door and asked her how long she would be. She told me that she had just started to take a shower. I had to go so badly, that I was going to run downstairs to the lower flat. When I started to go downstairs, she called out to me and said I could come in and use the bathroom and that I wouldn't disturb her, that she'd close the shower curtain. As I entered the bathroom, I had my eyes shut so that I would respect her and not look. I was attempting to situate myself over the toilet, with my eyes closed to take care of business, when she spoke again. I turned my head towards the shower and opened my eyes and realized the shower curtain was very thin and as the light from the window shined through, it showed this beautiful girl's body; *all of her assets*. At that point, my hormones were all over the place. I had never seen anything like this before, *not in person*, anyway and although I tried not to look, my eyes were fixed on her; it was impossible *not to look*. To my surprise, she pulled the curtain back and exposed herself to me completely. She said, *"It looks as if you need a shower, too. You're sweating."* At that point, I almost fainted. She asked me to get into the shower with her and so I did. She told me what to do and that's what I did. I didn't know what to do; while she helped me, then I said that I had to *pee*. She said, *'go ahead and pee.'* It was *coming…* I tried to pull back, but she held me tighter. I was thirteen and that was my first real experience with the opposite sex.

After she finally released me, she said *'do not tell anyone'* and asked

39

'was it good for me.' I do not remember what my response was in that moment, I was confused about what had just taken place.

Many times, before this, I would go down the street, to one of our friend's house into his garage and climb into the loft. We would look at the old Playboy and Hustler magazines that were left there, (we happened to run across them by accident one day while playing hide-and-go-seek), one of our friends was hard to find, so we went looking a little further for him and found him up in the loft, not saying a word. There were so many books up there, we could look at one a day for a year. They were old looking books and didn't have modern pictures. So, you see, to me, to see this young woman in the flesh was a bit overwhelming. Until this day, I have never talked to anyone about this, even to the boys in the locker rooms. Something happened that day, that I didn't understand at the time, but I do now. Shortly after that encounter, I began to increase masturbation after being with this young lady. I didn't know what I was doing as she showed me and it felt good, but can I tell you the truth, **"Everything that feels good to you, is not good for you"**

God created us with the ability to reproduce after our own kind, that means, He gave us a sexual appetite to fulfill his purpose in the earth. Sex is good if it wasn't we would not do it. God made it good. The human body was created to respond to sexual attraction *naturally*. Our sexual parts respond to smell, touch and sounds. It's a part of the sexual nature but in the right context and under the right conditions of marriage. What was wrong about what happened to me was I did not ask for this *to happen* and my body responded naturally and because it did; I believed *that I was bad* just like when I was nine years old and made to perform an act of perversion on another child. I also kept this to myself. The lie was that I wanted it, and liked it, but that was a lie from the pit of hell. I did not ask her to expose me to sex that day; she took advantage of my youthful innocence. That first encounter with this woman, (exposing me to a sexual relationship before my time), awakened *my body before my time*. Many of you, by one means or another was awakened before your time. It doesn't matter, if it was through incest, molestation, rape or any other form of sexual abuse, *your body was abused, misused and exploited.*

Before that encounter, all I knew was sports. In the days that followed, I would remember how she looked naked and what we had done, then I would imagine us doing it again and again. Then I would masturbate to fulfill the climax that I felt that day. Masturbation became a hobby for me. You may chuckle, but I was being controlled by the lusts of my flesh, and it was producing death, I couldn't tell anyone I had this problem, that I didn't understand and couldn't stop. There was a door now opened in my soul that I did not know how to shut. It took over my life and no woman were safe from my imagination. To look at me or to know me; you would not have known the person that I had become.

Through studying the word of God and courses taken and receiving godly counsel, today I am free! *"If the Son therefore shall make you free, ye shall be free indeed." (John 8:36) KJV.* For ye shall not only be delivered from the bondage of sin and its punishment, but made sons of God with and through Christ Jesus, and have an everlasting home with him in the Father's house. Do not be fooled by the enemy, *the thief cometh not, but for to steal and to kill, and to destroy. (John 10:10) KJV.* Yes, the devil is a thief! He comes to steal your innocence, your hopes and dreams. But for the grace of God and his mercy, *"I am come that you might have life, and that you might have it more abundantly."* (to the full – NIV) KJV. The word **abundantly** refers to a full, prosperous, healthy, wealthy and productive life. Allow the Lord to come in, forgive those who have hurt you deeply and set your soul free.

My freedom came as I believe in a *new report*, that I could forgive those that hurt and abused me. I did not have to live *in the shadows* anymore; that I could step into the light and be free. *Do you want to be free? Do you want to come out of that dark place?*

Ask the Lord today, to come in and help you, *forgive the unforgivable.*

NOTES

HOW DO YOU FEEL ABOUT THIS STORY

CHAPTER 12

SOMETHING BORROWED

I REMEMBER ONE PARTICULAR DAY before going to school, I decided that I was going to "*borrow*" money from my mother without her permission. I sneaked into her room and borrowed the money from her purse. I went outside and hid the money under a rock, so that I could pick it up on my way to school. I was smart enough not to keep the money on me because I had stolen before and was caught. This is what happened… church had let out on Sunday morning; all the kids would run to the corner store and buy a snack. This particular day, I had no snack money, so I took a bag of orange slices from the counter and stuck them in the front part of my pants and walked out of the store; yes, I *did not* get caught… I am home free. As I approached our car, I pushed the slices down so that I could sit down but of all days, my mother chooses this day to make me sit in the front seat between my older brother and her. As mom was about to pull off, she looked down at me and asked, "*Why did I go to the store when I had no money?* She looked at my pants and asked what was wrong with them. I replied, *nothing was wrong,* so my brother pulled my pants and the bag made a crackling sound, then he pulled the bag from my pants. Every one of my brothers and sisters were in the car, at the time, and my mother yelled at me and told me to go into the store and take the orange slices back and made me apologize to the owner. I was banned from the store that day. So, you see, I had a history of stealing. That is why I didn't keep the money on me when I took it from my mother's purse.

As I finished breakfast and about to set out to school, my mom realized that someone took money from her purse, she asked each of us about it and of course, I said that *I didn't take it.* She insisted the money was there and that she was going to get to the bottom of it! She told us that we were not going to leave for school until she got the money back; so we all sat there and looked at each other with stupid stares on our faces. Suddenly, mom opened the door and walked outside, then she came back inside after a moment and said, "*God was good.*" I was dumbfounded at that statement. But, once again, she asked... "*who stole the money*," and once again, we all said "*not me.*" She then showed us the $5.00 that was taken from her purse and said she knew who took it. She told us God showed her where the money was and showed her who took it. She looked at me and said, "*Andre you took the money.*" Still, I tried to deny it. Mom told us that God spoke to her and that He was real! From that day forward, I knew that God spoke to my mother because there's no way that she should have been able to know that I placed the money under a rock outside the door. That day, I knew God spoke to my mother, *either that* or she could look through walls.

You know God sees all and knows all; even when we think we're getting by with something, we are only fooling ourselves. God knows all about you and where you are at any given time and what you are doing and who you are with. **God sees all.**

Ephesians 4:28 KJV

Let the thief no longer steal, but rather let him labor, doing honest work with his own hands, so that he may have something to share with anyone in need.

Philippians 4:19 KJV

But my God shall supply all your needs according to Him riches in Glory by Christ Jesus.

I have learned to work with my hands and allow Father God to breath on what my hands find to do and that has produced wealth for my life and family.

Father God can do the same for you, He is no respecter of persons, what He does for me He'll do the same for you.

NOTES

HOW DO YOU FEEL ABOUT THIS STORY

_____

_____

_____

_____

_____

_____

_____

_____

_____

_____

_____

_____

_____

_____

_____

_____

_____

_____

_____

_____

CHAPTER 13

HIS THOUGHTS TOWARDS ME

ALL DURING HIGH SCHOOL, I was a handful for my parents. I wouldn't do my schoolwork and I had a lot of problems that I did not want to deal with. One day, mom told one of the men at church, that I needed someone to talk to. She told me that this man needed to talk to me because she was unable to get through to me. Maybe this man could. I didn't think that anything was wrong with me, *but I was wrong*. This man's name was Brother Copeland and he was working with a ministry called Urban Christian Ministries (UCM), located on Jefferson Street in Buffalo, New York. Brother Copeland took me out and talked to me about his life and how God had blessed him. I listened and for the first time, *I really listened*. He took me to one of UCM's Camps that they had every summer. We went to Camp Bliss, which was located up in the mountains. Time after time, Brother Copeland would pick me up and do various things with other young men and myself. We would go camping in the mountains, swimming and on other trips. As he began to take time to help me, I realized that I needed to do better in school.

In my senior year, I really pushed hard to do my best. I worked hard to be able to graduate. Graduation time came and the report cards arrived. I was surprised to find out that I was unable to graduate with my class because I didn't pass a general math class, in my *freshman year. That really set me off*! I was so mad that I was unable to graduate. I was told that I had to return to Burgard the next year. Because I tried so hard to make up for lost time, during my senior year and didn't make it, I told them *what they could do with next year*. I was disappointed in myself and mad at the school system. I did not receive a high school diploma and I didn't care. I dropped out of school because I was embarrassed and ashamed. Many people talked to me about returning to school, but I refused to go back. I remembered my mother saying to me that it would hurt me when my friends graduated and I didn't hear her then, but it rang true that day. *It hurt like a knife in my heart.*

After a few weeks had gone by, my dad talked to me and asked me of my plans for my life. I told him something, though, I am not sure what I told him; but he told me that if I don't get a diploma or GED, I would not be able to even get a janitor's job cleaning floors. I pondered this for a few weeks and went and signed up for the GED exam. I took the exam and passed with *flying colors!* The people at EOC asked why I dropped out of school. I told them what happened and they wished me luck in life and told me that I could use the GED to get a job. My dad asked me or rather he told me a few weeks after I received my scores from EOC that I needed to apply for a job because he was not going to let me sit around the house without one.

Basically, he was telling me to get off my lazy butt and get a job! I went out that Monday morning, set to find a job. That was easy enough, I thought. Yes, it would be a piece of cake. Everywhere I went, though, I was told that I needed more education or that I needed experience. After going from place to place, this became tiring, so I stopped. I asked myself, "How do I get experience if no one will hire me?" Finally, I put in an application for Top's Supermarket and was called in for an interview. A woman looked at my application and I could see the look in her eyes. Her eyes said, "this poor kid." She asked me about my work history and I told her that I had none. When she asked why, I told her that I was always told that I needed experience. How could I have experience if no one would hire me? She told me that she would give me a chance. When she asked when could I start I told her any time, and I started that weekend restocking shelves, I started my first real job. My good friend, Ronald Jr., also applied and was hired.

My first job was a key point in my life and I was finally able to make some money. For the first couple of weeks, I worked my rump off, lifting boxes and stocking shelves all during the night. This was not like I thought it would be. Payday finally came and I was getting *my first paycheck.* I was so excited. My supervisor gave me my check. Lo and behold, when I opened it, I realized that there was only about $64.00 after two weeks of hard work. I almost threw the check back at him. I thought there had to be some mistake. My supervisor told me that there was no mistake; *taxes, union dues and some of everything else were taken out of my check*, this was a rude awakening to the *real world of adulthood*. During that time, I was also enrolled in Houghton College during the day and was taking Bible classes. UCM had a program that would allow me to take classes, so I did. I realized that Tops was not the place for me. There was too much hard work and not enough pay, but I stuck it out for a while. One day, I could not take it anymore, so I just didn't go back to Tops. *I quit with no notice.*

I looked for another job and found one at AM & A's clothing store in the Southgate Plaza in West Seneca, New York. This was great, because Houghton College was just above the hill from the plaza where I worked. Everything was great except for one thing. How would I get from Buffalo to West Seneca every day for work and school? One day after classes, one of the students asked me where I was staying and I told him how I traveled back and forth on the bus each day. He told me that I could stay in his room on the days that I had to work and attend school because he had an extra bed in his room. This went on for a few weeks and then I dropped out of college. I was no longer in college, so I quit my job at AM&A's. I quit school because I felt that I couldn't cut it. I really had low self-esteem and seemed unable to complete what I started. *I would abandon everything, just like my parents abandoned me.*

My life was like a roller coaster at that time. I didn't know which way was up. I took another job working at the Buffalo Convention Center. I was in the Food Service Department. That was a fun job. All of my friends from church were there and all of us were hired, *so the fun began*. We would prepare meals for the conventions along with the chefs. The only part that I didn't like was the clean up after the conventions. The pots were so big; you could stand in them to clean them out. That was hard work.

I moved from my dad's house and in with my friend Bill, who was there for me, when I was going through hard times as a youth. We lived on Arden Street in Buffalo and stayed in the upstairs flat. I had a nice room and that was a blessing for me. Two other guys also stayed with us. We had many good times there. I stayed there for some time and *then moved out on my own*. This was an experience that I was not ready for, but I thought I was. My apartment was on Chelsea Place in Buffalo. My landlord was a wonderful man, a good Deacon… *who has since gone on to glory*. Nevertheless, he was a praying man, too. One day after Sunday service, he approached me and asked, "*Son, do you need some place to stay?*" I replied, "*Yes, how did you know?*" He said, "*that the Lord showed him that I was in need.*"

You see, even when you do not know that God is looking out for you, *He is!* He happened to have an apartment available and asked me to take a look at it. That evening, I went by and decided to take the apartment. It was small and had only one bedroom, but it would be mine. I had all of the utilities turned on and I was proud to be on my own.

Brother Copeland was the manager of a place called the Budget Shop. It was a second hand, third hand and even forth hand store and had whatever other people didn't want. I would help him out by delivering and picking up furniture. Because I helped out there, he would allow me to pick out clothes, shirts, shoes, coats and more. That is how I was able to furnish my apartment. Things went well for a while and then all hell broke loose.

I quit my job, now, I had no money and as you know… I soon found out, with no money, the bills didn't get paid and when the bills don't get paid, the utilities get cut off. The good Deacon/Landlord, thankfully, was a very longsuffering, patient man. He would tell me to pay rent whenever I could. Then, my gas was cut off and all I could hear was my dad's voice saying, "*Son, it's not easy out there.*" I was grown and I was smart and moved out anyway. When things got so bad that I didn't have much money, I would go to the store and buy the ramen noodles that were four for one dollar. I became king of the noodles! Finally, I broke down and swallowed my pride and went to apply for public assistance. I was too proud to go back to my father's house because I didn't want him to know that he was right. I was messed up!

As a result of quitting my job, I was denied public assistance; and told that I was not out of work long enough. The woman there did help me with emergency food stamps though and that helped me for a moment. Still, I had no money to have my gas turned back on. I was on food stamps for about one month and I couldn't take it anymore. I felt that I had to find a job, so I went job-hunting again. This time, I applied and no one would give me a job. I got frustrated and I told God that I didn't want to do bad things to get money. I told Him that I needed a job. I spoke with my friend Bill and told him about my situation and he said he had a room, to come stay with him, *again*. He had moved onto Thornton Avenue in Buffalo. I later applied for a job at McDonald's on Bailey Avenue. The manager, there took the application and asked me to sit down, she told me that she needed a person and asked did I want the job. I said, *"Yes,"* and I started that job the following day. I worked this job and became shift manager in one month. I was managing the afternoon shift.

Even though I had to go through this time in my life, I still seen the hand of the Lord working for me in it all. Be encouraged and know that God is still working it out for you! ***"His thoughts for you are good and not evil to give you a hope and a future." (Jeremiah 29:11)***

NOTES

HOW DO YOU FEEL ABOUT THIS STORY

_____

_____

_____

_____

_____

_____

_____

_____

_____

_____

_____

_____

_____

_____

_____

_____

_____

_____

_____

_____

_____

_____

_____

_____

CHAPTER 14

LINES THAT SEPARATE

I ATTENDED *BURGARD VOCATIONAL HIGH School*, the school of *Auto Mechanics and Aviation*. I went to Burgard, not because I thought that I could be an auto mechanic, but because some of the other brothers from Bethesda Full Gospel Church went there and because they were there, I followed. This wasn't a hard choice, because I didn't have many choices, with my grades; which were not good enough to go to an academic school and back then, they were sending you to a vocational school. I wasn't good enough to get in Hutchinson Technical school and my grades weren't good enough to get in Bennett High. Thus, my freshman year began and I walked through the *front doors* of *Burgard*. I could not believe that I was actually in high school. You can imagine that as freshmen, people are the object of many foolish pranks and it was no different at Burgard. One morning, some of the black kids caught one of the white boys on the bus. They felt they were going to initiate this poor kid, but they took it a little too far. They took him off of the bus that was headed for school, ran him up a telephone pole, egged him and wrote on him. Afterwards, they left him hanging there.

That was not a great morning at school. We were getting ready for classes, when I heard a loud noise coming from the hallway, next to the *Shop* rooms. I went out to investigate. As I approached the rear of the building, where the shouting was coming from, I couldn't believe my eyes. The hall was filled with students carrying bats, chains, crowbars, knives, tire irons and anything that could be picked up. The white students were on one side and the blacks and Hispanic students were on the other. People were shouting racial slurs back and forth. '*Nigger, spick, dago, honkie, white trash, speck, your mother this, your mother that*!' The teachers and the security guards came and were able to get between the angry mob. They tried to find out what was wrong. I was very confused and didn't know what to do or say. I didn't know whose side to take... you had to have been there; you had to take a side. My problem was that some of my best friends were white and they attended Burgard and was also in the crowd. My church at that time was under the leadership of Pastor William White, Jr. He was a white preacher presiding over a 98% black congregation. Pastor White was a man that I respected very deeply and his sons were some of my best friends. So, you can imagine the dilemma that I was in. I chose to go to the side of the ones I thought represented me because they looked like me. My white friends went to the other side. On that day, we made a statement that was loud and clear. Though we worshipped together, *side by side*, there was still a line that divided us. *That line did not start with us, but we were a part of that line that day.*

Thank God no one got seriously hurt *that day*. Things settled down. The police came and talked to several students and that was the end of that. Though the tension was in the air for some time thereafter, nothing reared up. Things seemed to be back to a chaotic normal. The Pastor's son and I never said anything after that day about what had happened. After a few months, I realized that I didn't like that school. I told my guidance counselor that I was unhappy with Burgard and wanted to leave. He advised me to stay and give it a little more time. He told me that I didn't see all that Burgard had to offer, so I did as he suggested. Sometimes as I reflect, I believe what happened to me, after our conversation, (with my staying at Burgard), was the biggest mistake of my life.

Exedus 32:26 KJV

Then Moses stood in the gate of the camp, and said who is on the Lord side? Let him come unto me.

That day in the hall way I had a choice to make, I made that choice, was it the right choice? Each person will have to answer that for themselves. I know now what I did not know then is that truly the only side I should take is the Lord's side. Will you make the right choice today and choose the Lord's side?

NOTES

HOW DO YOU FEEL ABOUT THIS STORY

CHAPTER 15

MURDEROUS HEART

THIS MORNING, IN PARTICULAR, I arrived at school and entered my homeroom. I noticed that we had a substitute teacher. I do not remember his name, but he was about 6'1 and about 140-150 pounds. He was clean looking, had a low haircut and was neatly dressed. He was there all day. My last class was shop and my homeroom teacher was also my shop teacher. The substitute was still there. He knew nothing about automobiles except for the fact that he drove one. As I was leaving class that day to go home, the substitute asked me to stay for a moment. Naturally, I thought I was in trouble. Before that last class, I had taken gym and was very sweaty. I was unable to take a shower after gym because of the time restraints. So, I had to go to shop sweating. I had no shirt on… I had to just air dry. The substitute teacher asked me if I had a job and I told him, "*No.*" He said that he needed some strong young men to help him move some boxes at his house. He then squeezed my arms and said that they were firm and strong. That's what he needed. I agreed to take the job. I was proud that I was firm and in good shape. On that particular night, we had Bible study at church. Normally, I would attend Bible study with my mother, but when I arrived home from school, I was so excited about the offer to make a little money. I told my mom about this and she said, '*okay,*' but I was to go to church when I was done. The hour was approaching for me to go, so I left early; this way I could arrive at the substitute's teacher's house on time. I arrived at the address that was given to me and rang the doorbell. An older gentleman opened the door and asked me if I was there for his son. I answered, "*Yes.*" The man let me in and directed me up the stairs to the second floor; there were five older men there along with the substitute teacher. He introduced me as one of his students. I took a seat and waited for a while. Finally, I asked the substitute where the other boys were, who was supposed to come and help. He told me that he didn't know, but that I would suffice. I was offered something to eat, but I refused. I told the substitute that I had to go to church, so I needed to get on with moving what he needed. He asked me to stand up and to walk to the center of the room. So I did. He approached me and rubbed my arms and told me to pull down my pants. I didn't respond, so he told me to pull down my pants again. I was so afraid of those men in that room, I froze. I have never been so afraid before. Slowly, I pulled my pants down and he took hold of my Johnson and sexually abused me. I was not penetrated, though. I believe for many years, that I was better off because I was not penetrated, but I tell you today, that I still had the same trauma as one who was. While this was going on, the other men who was there… did nothing but watch as if it was a show and I was the main attraction. I was paralyzed; unable to move. I could not believe that this was happening to me. Afterwards, the substitute looked at me and told me, "You are still a man and I am not gay, because I did this to you. (*As if that was some consolation prize!*) I fixed my clothing and walked down the stairs and outside the front door. I walked from there to my church, *Bethesda at Main and Utica Street.* Bethesda was having Bible study and my mother was there, someone went and told her I was outside crying; she put her arms around me and asked what was wrong. I don't remember what I told her, but it was not the truth. I intended to tell her, but because of the rush of emotions of embarrassment and shame I felt… I didn't tell her I gave her some story, but not the truth. (*So often when we are abused by someone we feel guilt and shame and that causes us to hide behind a lie*). I went into service that night with anger so strong that I could kill someone.

The next day I set out to kill this teacher, his father and anyone else that was in the home at that time and with reckless abandonment, I prepared a molotov cocktail. I walked up and down the street looking for the house of this teacher. I had something in my hand to destroy many lives that day, but as I walked to find the house, I could not find it. I know the house… I know where I was; but I could not find the house and after several moments frustrated and angry that I couldn't find the house, I just left. **(They lived to see another day)**. Because it was the weekend, I had a lot of time to rehearse this event in my mind. I played it over and over, in my mind, and told myself that it was my fault. *I believed it was my fault.* I was in this all alone and I was tormented. Back in school, the next Monday morning, I found my regular teacher there. Class went on as usual, but the *Andre'* that was there before was not the same *Andre'* in class that day. At least for me, that *Andre'* ceased to be.

The anger in me was now even greater than ever. I decided that *Andre'* was not going to get hurt anymore. Protecting myself and taking care of myself were now my goals. This was the third time, I had been sexually abused and it won't happen again. This event caused me to feel there was something terribly wrong with me. I had no understanding of *homosexuality* and no understanding of the lifestyle of homosexuals; but because of the abuse, I felt that I must have been gay, too. I didn't want to be gay and I told myself that many times. Many thoughts ran through my mind at that time. *I was very confused and angry.* After some time, that anger turned into rage. After being sexually abused for a third time, I began to have thoughts about committing suicide. I had it all planned out in my mind. There where thoughts that no one would really know and no one really cared *anyway.* I felt neither of my parents cared because they didn't help me. I decided to just end it. There was a voice in my head telling me to go ahead and kill myself, to stop thinking about it and just do it, *"Take the razor and slit your wrists the way you saw it on television. It's easy."* I thought about it for a moment and that passed. I didn't attempt suicide, but I felt that no one was there to help me. I was crying out for help, but no one heard me. *How could I expect them to know*? I felt that my mother should have known that something was wrong. She was a woman of God; she even said that the Lord speaks to her. I wondered why didn't the Lord speak to her about this. Thoughts of suicide haunted me daily after this. What was there to live for; my life is over and the worst thing that could ever happen to me indeed *did* and *my life is over.* This invasion affected me in my daily life. I began to hate 'gays.' I just wanted to punch or beat down any of them that crossed my path. I felt they didn't deserve to live. This thing took away my peace and my joy. I set in my heart to do harm.

It wasn't until many years later, in an inner healing class, after receiving a level of healing, the Lord spoke to me and let me know that that day I determined in my heart to murder those men in that house, he had dispatched an angel on assignment to cloak that home so that I couldn't see it to carry out the plan of the devil. He told me that was not my destiny that was not the plan He has for me. That day, I realized that Father God had a plan for me and it was not to take a life but to *SAVE LIFE.*

Romans 12:19

Beloved, never avenge yourselves, but leave it to the wrath of God, for it is written, "Vengeance is mine, I will repay, says the Lord."

Let the Lord fight for you He has never lost a battle

NOTES

HOW DO YOU FEEL ABOUT THIS STORY

_____

_____

_____

_____

_____

_____

_____

_____

_____

_____

_____

_____

_____

_____

_____

_____

_____

_____

_____

_____

_____

_____

_____

_____

_____

_____

CHAPTER 16

THE MAN I AM

HIGH SCHOOL WAS INTERESTING. BURGARD VHS was a school of mostly boys; there were only about twelve girls there. I couldn't understand why a girl would attend Burgard to become a *grease monkey*. That's what we were called, *grease monkeys*. The distractions that Bennett High and the other schools had; we didn't have at Burgard. There was no one to impress or compete with. The only problem that we did have was that some of the students felt very comfortable being with the same sex. It was not a problem *per se*, and those students stayed to themselves.

One day, someone approached me in gym and asked me or told me rather, that I was caught on the ramps kissing a guy. I was outraged at this accusation and wanted to know where the rumor came from. The fellow who approached me continued to say that he didn't know that I was gay. I tried to defend myself, but of course, that was a big joke. All day long, I was defending myself from that rumor. "*Why me?*" I wondered, "*Why me?!*" Over the next few days, there was a burning anger inside of me and I said to myself, "*I hate gay people.*" Finally, I found out that it was all a mistake. There *were* two guys kissing on the third-floor ramp and one of their names was *Andre'* and that is how the rumor got started.

I was on the football team, the basketball team and ran track. I was very athletic, but not academically inclined. I was all into sports at that time, but not really into girls. I just didn't have the time. There were guys always talking about girls and about what they had done with them. Most of this talk was false, that's just how guys pumped themselves up in the locker rooms. I'm sure this happened all across America and across the world too. One day, as the guys talked, they asked me whom I had been with. They called me *Dre'* for short and wanted to know. So, they probed, "*You never talk about girls, Dre'... Are you gay or something?*" After that statement, I felt that I had to prove that I was a man. You see, those words provoked me. I was already struggling with my '*identity*' as a man; now it seemed as if those words from the guys shook me to my core. I went out and began sleeping around. I decided that every girl that I went out with from that point on, I would '*make out*' with them or *at least try*. I had to prove that I was not gay and that I was as much of a man as the next guy. If having sex would make me a man, then I was going to be a man. Of course, I didn't understand what being a man was all about. But, as you can see, because of the hurt that I felt inside of me, I allowed that hurt to lead me to the decisions that I made. I left several women *scarred* because of my hurts and wounds.

It took quite some time for me to realize, that I was trying to prove to the boy in me that I was a man, when all along I was a man. I allowed what happened to me, lie *within* me and caused me to believe that because these terrible things took place, in my life, that I was someone different.

The circumstances in our lives do not make us who we are! We are what God created us to be. In my attempts to heal myself, I hurt others. If a clock is broken, it can't fix itself; but it needs the clock maker to repair it. So, it is with ourselves… We cannot fix ourselves; we need the Creator to put us back together again.

As long as I tried to fix myself, I continually made a mess of my life and hurt others at the same time. Stop trying to fix yourself! You too, can call on Father God, as I did and ask Him to fix you.

You do not have to prove who you are, God made you perfect and He does not make any mistakes. We at times get messed up through the abuses and the wounding of our past, but God made you who you are and the right gender. Ask God "who am I" I guarantee if you will ask with honest heart He will answer.

NOTES

HOW DO YOU FEEL ABOUT THIS STORY

CHAPTER 17

FAMILY SECRETS

ONE OF THE MOST SUBTLE weapons the devil has in his arsenal is secrets, (family secrets and/or personal secrets). **"What happens in the family, stays in this family."** This saying is not necessarily spoken out loud, but it is surely manifested in probably all of our families. My family is not exempt. Many years ago, when I was about 17 years old, working for the Mayor's Summer Youth Program, at the St. Augustine Center on Fillmore Avenue near Northland Street in Buffalo, New York, I had just started the program and my job was as an exterior housing specialist; we would walk the streets with a form that had addresses on them. We had to fill out the form based on the condition of the home. I really enjoyed this job. This one particular day, myself and a few other young men, around my age, were sitting; waiting to get our assignment, when a beautiful young lady walked through the door and went up the stairs to an upper office, (*that area was off limits to us*) so we never went up there; we all watched her glide up those stairs full of grace. We began to act as most youthful boys do and started to talk silly and how could we get to the girl. We looked at each other to see who had the better chance and made a sport of it; *a game* where each one of us should try to talk to her and see if she gave us the time of day. I was *chosen* to go first. I creeped up the stairs to the upper office area and there she was as 'pretty as she could be' sitting at her desk working. It seemed as though things were moving in slow motion. I told myself that she would not go out with me and I turned to walk back down the stairs to save myself from sheer humiliation. I do not know about other ethnic group women, but a black woman can tear a brother down, peel him back like a union and toss him to the curb. As I turned around, she asked… *"Can I help you?"* I stuttered and trembled, but said, *"yes,"* that I needed some paperwork, thinking quick on my feet. She said that I could get that paperwork from my supervisor downstairs. I knew this, but I had to say something intelligent. I was just about to walk down the stairs, when she asked, *was there anything else I needed* and from somewhere, I do not know… out of these lips, I asked her if she was busy that night. She looked at me with surprise on her face, paused for a moment, I braced myself for the tongue lashing, when she said, *"No, I am not."* I was so shocked that I could have wet in my pants. I then asked if she would like to go see a movie at the Downtown Cinema and she said, *"Sure."* We exchanged cell numbers and she gave me her address. I said, I'd be there to pick her up at six p.m. that evening.

I came down stairs and told the boys, that I got a date for tonight. They did not believe me and *'why would she go out with you'* and that's how we left it; because the other boys were too scared to go upstairs and ask.

I went out to do my job and the first house I came to; near the corner of Northland and Fillmore Avenue was one that myself along with two of the other workers had been looking at; since this house according to the paperwork, needed to have had several improvements; but it didn't. So, as we stood in front of the house, an older man came out of the front door, waving a large caliber hand gun, asking us what were we doing and to get out of there; we ran of course, for our lives, that day.

After this ordeal, my work day was cut short and I was released to go home, for the day. I went home, with such a big smile on my face, because I had a date with a beautiful young lady and I had expectations. I expected to score that night. I took a shower, put on my best clothes and cologne and started for the address that was given to me. I arrived at address by human power, okay… *I walked there.* As I approached the house, I saw a few boys playing football in front of the house. I walked up to the house, when I heard my named called, but I was confused because I didn't know anyone on this Street and I had never been over to this address before; *so, who could possibly know my name?* One of the boys walked over to me and actually called me *by name* and told me *his name,* then he asked, *'what I was doing over there,'* and I told him I was coming to pick up my date. He then looked at me, rather strangely and asked, *'you came to pick up a date at this address?'* I said, *'Yes!'* He asked what the name of the girl was… so, I told him and he busted out into uncontrollable laughter. I was really confused *and* annoyed at him. I didn't realize this was one of my cousins, that I had not seen since I was very young, but he somehow recognized me. He said, *'I'll take you in,'* so, I followed him into the house and as we walked in he yelled, for *"Nanna,"* an older woman came out and my cousin introduced me and even said whose son I was; called my father's name. She looked at me and said, *"Oh my God, I have not seen you since you were a little boy."* I was saying to myself, *'Well, I never seen you before.'* Nanna hugged me and asked, 'how did I find her house and before I could say anything, my cousin blurted out that I was there to take the young lady out on a date. Nanna then said, *"Oh my Lord,"* then she told me to have a seat. As I was being seated, she called for the young lady and *she* appeared from the room more gorgeous than ever; my heart was racing and my breathing was shallow. I just starred at her without blinking. She smiled and asked, *'What was going on?'* Nanna told her to have a seat as well, and she looked just as confused as I was, while she sat down in the chair facing me. Nanna asked her, *"Do you know who this boy is?"* and she said, *'Yes, he works at St. Augustine Center.'* Nanna said, *"No, do you know whose son this is?"* and she said, *'No'...* how would she; as we had honestly just met. At that moment, both of our worlds changed. Nanna said that I was the son of her father... *"this is your brother!"* We both set there for a moment, *in shock.* She suddenly got up and ran away to her room, crying and never came back out while I was there. I had a short conversation with them and left for home. The next morning, when I arrived for work, the boys started to laugh and point their fingers, saying, *"Man, she said she turned you down."* I wanted to say something to protect myself, but I didn't. I really do not remember what I said to those guys after that but, it all settled down and we went about our business. I could not tell them what *really happened* and I certainly didn't want to embarrass her *any further.* She and I never spoke again and she avoided me from that day on. At this time in my life, I was still trying to prove that I was man, so like a lion on the prowl, I was looking for my next young lady to conquer. I was full of *lust and anger.*

I found out many years later that my dad had other children around the same age as I was, but no one ever told me; so me being a young boy with expectations, on my mind, was about to possibly make a big mistake with who I thought was my sister; but to finally find out the truth, my father had a son who had a sister who was not of my father's blood, a different father, this left me even more angrier at my biological (father) than I was prior to this new information. The thought of what could have taken place, just sends shivers down my spine.

I encourage you to speak to those who are keeping such secrets in *your family*. Keep them from your children no longer. It is more damaging to them as they get older. I have heard people say, "*I am protecting them.*" Is that so? Just know that the real truth is that you are still protecting yourself. It's not about them at all… man up, woman up, the old saying, "*honesty is the best policy.*" Stop lying to them and to yourself. ***The Lord detests lying lips, but He delights in people who are trustworthy. (Proverbs 12:22).***

NOTES

HOW DO YOU FEEL ABOUT THIS STORY

_____

_____

_____

_____

_____

_____

_____

_____

_____

_____

_____

_____

_____

_____

_____

_____

_____

_____

_____

_____

_____

_____

_____

_____

_____

CHAPTER 18

BELIEVING MY OWN LIE

I MADE THE DECISION, FOR the first time, to visit Mississippi and to meet my mother. I told some of my friends and they thought I was crazy. They said that if she wanted to see me or know about me, she would have made the first move. I thought about that and felt that they were right. I didn't give her away; she gave me away. I began to get angry all over again. I talked with others and they told me that it was a good thing to look for my mother, if that was what I really wanted to do. Throughout all of this, I never told my parents who loved me and had taken care of me all of my life. They were the ones I loved and respected, but I was ashamed and felt that I would be hurting their feelings, so I kept the news from them. Later, I called Mississippi and talked to my biological mother and told her that I wanted to meet her and my sisters. The next week, I took the money that I had from my job and put it aside for my ticket to Mississippi. Still, I hadn't told my parents. All week I saw my schoolmates leave for college. One of my best friends was leaving for college as well. My friend was headed for RIT. I was ashamed that I was not going to college, so conveniently, I told my friend that I was going to Jackson State College in Mississippi. All week long, I told people that I was going away to college. It was really crazy, but *I began to believe it myself!* I told it as if it were true. That Sunday morning came and we went to church. I planned to leave that afternoon to go to Mississippi. I told my friends that I was going to miss them and one of them told the pastor. The pastor told the congregation that I was leaving to go to Mississippi and that they should give me an offering to help me on my journey. Our church was like that; they would give for a cause. That day, they gave me $250.00 and that was truly a blessing. Sadly, this was the first time my parents found out about my trip and that hurt them very much. That afternoon, I went to the bus station with my girlfriend, who was there to see me off. As I was waiting for the bus, my best friend was leaving for college at the same time. His bus was next to my bus. He was getting on the Rochester bus and I was getting on the Mississippi bus. My friend and I hugged and said that we would see each other in four years. *I carried the lie about college for many years and I am ashamed of that.*

My parents didn't show up, at the bus station, that day because they were very hurt. Off, I went to Mississippi. I had a stopover in Tennessee and while there; a gentleman who asked me if I was headed for college approached me. I said, *"Yes."* He asked where and I told him Jackson State College. He told me that he was looking for some investors that were in college. He wanted some smart kids to invest in a money making program. After ten minutes, he had my $250.00. I can't even remember what the scam was, but he said that he would send me my share of the profit to Jackson State College and I believed him. You must understand that I was really messed up.

First, I took the money that the church had given and I gave it away, secondly and most disturbingly, I told this man that I was going to Jackson State College and for him to send me the money there. I was so mixed up in this lie that I lost all sense of reality around me. *That was bondage to be sure!* And, that thing had me bad! I was so messed up that after I got on my bus, I still didn't get it. I told myself that maybe this man would find me somehow. *Well, I can safely say that he has not found me yet.* But, if he happens to read this book and remembers me, and if he is now a Christian and feels as though he did me wrong, he can send me the $250.00 with interest and that would be okay with me.

I told that lie out of shame of failure. Many people have to deal with the shame of *failure.* That is a bad seed and when it is planted, it will bring forth a destructive harvest. Some of you who have been adopted can identify with what I am talking about. There are certain characteristics that come with being adopted and one is a sense of failure. A sense that I am not good enough *to do this or that.* Also, there is a fear of starting something because one fears that he will fail. *Therefore, he or she fails to do.* This is what I was dealing with. I was afraid of failure and afraid that people would know that I was a failure; so I hid behind the story that I was going to attend college. I held on to this lie that I was going to Jackson State College on a *Track* scholarship, for your information, I have never even seen Jackson State College, only from the outside passing by while I was in Jackson, Mississippi staying with my biological mom.

Sometimes we get so caught up in our fantasy world of lies that we become lost. I was so lost in this *lie*, to the point, that I gave a stranger $250.00 to invest with the belief that he would send my dividends to a college that I was never attending; *not only that*, but that somehow the money would find its way to me... *that's messed up.*

Be who you are, do not pretend to be anything else but who God created you to be. The real you don't have to pretend.

I Timothy 6:10

For the love of money is the root of all kinds of evil. Some people, eager for money, have wandered from the faith and pierced themselves with many griefs.

NOTES

HOW DO YOU FEEL ABOUT THIS STORY

_____

_____

_____

_____

_____

_____

_____

_____

_____

_____

_____

_____

_____

_____

_____

_____

_____

_____

_____

_____

_____

_____

CHAPTER 19

FACE TO FACE

MISSISSIPPI WAS A BEAUTIFUL PLACE. It was not what I expected it to be like. When I arrived at the bus station, I looked around for someone who would be there to pick me up. There were two young ladies standing with another lady and they seemed to be looking for someone. I looked further because I was looking for my mother and two little girls. No one fit that description. I only saw these three young women. As I waited, one of the girls approached me and asked was my name *Andre'*. I said, "*Yes.*" She hugged me and said that she was my sister. I almost fainted because she was a big girl now. I had forgotten the years that passed by and still expected to see little girls. They all came over and my mother hugged me and kissed me and that was one great moment for me. I went with them and we arrived at a house in the hills outside of Jackson, not far from the city. They showed me the room that I was to stay in and I laid on the bed and fell asleep. When I woke up, I was told that *I slept for two days*. I thought they were joking, but they were not. It was two days later when I woke up. The bus ride took 34 hours. I would suggest to anyone going to Mississippi to not take the bus. That was the longest, most miserable ride, I have ever taken.

My expectations were to meet them and leave, but it didn't happen quite that way. As I got to know them a little better and found out about my sisters, I realized that they were so very different from each other. They were twins, but were not identical. That's what had me so confused at the bus station. I was looking for my mother and identical twins. My mother was great and I enjoyed just sitting and talking to her. I asked her questions about the past. I didn't ask anything really pressing, just questions about the past. My questions were not answered to my satisfaction; it seemed to be many holes in the story, yet I accepted what she said but not satisfied. My mother said that she was sad because of that decision, but that *God knew what needed to be done.* Yet the anger in me still lingered on. I found out today that the statement that she made (*God knew what he had to do*) was the truth.

This lasted for about a week or so. I got to meet my mother's mother and her husband and they were a charming couple. I didn't remember my mother's mother at all, so she was a pleasant sight. As time went on, I began working in their beauty salon. My grandmother and mother were beauticians and owned their own shop. They also sold hair products. My grandmother and a chemist developed a hair solution for curls and they sold that solution around the country and also used it in their shop. That was pretty exciting to me. I would help her husband deliver this product to the towns nearby and also would have the products delivered by UPS to the rest of the country.

Many good things came out of my visit to Mississippi. I met some great people. I met cousins that I never knew about. I learned of my great grandfather, my mother's father and how he acquired the land that they lived on. *He was a horse trainer for his 'master' and was the best in the area. He bought his freedom through the earnings of racing those horses. Later, he bought some land, 3,000 acres for one dollar per acre. He raised horses on that land and continued racing them for a living.* I talked to some of my cousins and learned that I had *Indian* blood in me. I learned that my great grandfather's mother was an *Indian*. They showed me pictures of my relatives and it was amazing to see these people and to learn that I came from a proud line of people.

I loved Mississippi. One day, I was playing basketball, with some kids who lived down the road. They didn't have pavement on the streets like we do here in the North, so we played on the worn down dirt. There was a pole and backboard like we have in the North but this was the first time, that I played outside. We would normally play in a gym that was air conditioned, but this day, I stepped outside and brought a hand towel full of ice wrapped up, so I could eat some as I played. We played one game. I don't even remember if I won or not, but I do remember that the game took about 20 minutes. After it was over, I went over to my towel and it was bone dry! There was no ice. I told the kids to stop playing and asked who took my ice. They said that they didn't, but that the heat was so hot that it dried up the cloth. They told me that the heat there was not like the heat back home. Needless to say, that was the last time I played outside again. I don't like heat anyway.

I was in Mississippi for about a year and a half. One day, I got real sick. I was so sick that I was unable to sit down because my gluteus maximums were hurting so badly. My mother took me to the free clinic to see what was wrong. I went in and waited for the doctor to call me. After he called me, the normal procedures were done. I had to remove my clothing and put on a robe. The nurse told me that the doctor would be with me in a moment. That moment took quite some time. Finally, the doctor came in and asked me what seemed to be my problem. I told him and he told me to turn over. He checked me and said that I had what looked like a boil. He told me that he had to check me further. So, he stuck his fingers where no one has ever gone before. I was quite in pain! I asked him what was he doing and he said that he had to see if there was anything else going on up there. I know it was his job, but I really felt violated. After he was done, he told me that I had a pilonidal cyst it's an abnormal skin growth located at the tailbone that contains hair and skin and it had roots like a tree.

He told me I would need surgery to remove the cyst! Those were strong words to hear! Surgery! Unfortunately, I had no insurance in Mississippi, and I was told they would be unable to perform the surgery there. I left the clinic and walked to my mother's hair shop. The shop was only around the corner from the clinic. I told my mother the news and she told me there were no free hospitals in Mississippi. I called Buffalo, New York and told my dad that I needed surgery and I had to return. My dad told me he would check to see if the insurance on his job could cover me.

NOTES

HOW DO YOU FEEL ABOUT THIS STORY

CHAPTER 20

HELP IS ON THE WAY

I SET OFF BACK TO Buffalo and told everyone I would be back after the surgery. I had a *"Little Philly."* That's urban slang for a *little sweet heart*; I met while in Mississippi. I wanted her to come too. The day I left Mississippi was sad; I knew I would deeply miss them. When I left, I took all of my clothing and belongings with me even though I told everyone that I was coming back. I left no signs that I would be returning, though. I didn't know it then, *but I was not coming back.*

The train ride was terrible. I could not sit or stand because the pain was so great. I could hardly bear it and felt sick all over. One of the stops that the train made was in Chicago. I knew that my Aunt Helen lived in Chicago. I was there one time before with my family. I didn't know her address or even the street, but I was desperate. I got off the train in Chicago and got on a bus with my entire luggage. I rode the bus for a while and then got off the bus and started walking. No one knew that I would be in Chicago, so no one was there looking for me. I was in so much pain, that I cannot even describe it. As I walked a few blocks, a little boy came out of nowhere and asked if he could help me with my luggage, my response was *"I am okay,"* but he grabbed my suitcase and struggled to carry it anyway, for about two blocks, no less. I looking down the street, when I saw a young boy crossing the street who looked like my cousin *Hakeem*. I yelled at him with all of the strength that I could muster, he turned to see who called him and saw me. He ran over to me and asked *"what are you doing in Chicago?"* I began to tell him what happened to me. Hakeem took my bags. I turned to give the boy $5.00 and while my suitcase was there; the boy was gone, just as fast as he came, *he disappeared.* I'll talk about the little boy in another chapter.

I was only a few doors away from where my aunt lived and I didn't know it. My cousin took my bags and told me to get into the house quickly. I asked him, 'why,' but he said, 'just get in quickly.' He had left school that day to come home for lunch when he heard me call his name.

His school was just across the street from his home. We went into the house and he asked me whether I knew that I was in *blood territory*. I didn't know what he was talking about, so he told me to look out the window and I did. Standing on the corner was some boys and they all had on red bandanas. My cousin told me that they were watching me because I had on a blue shirt. Wearing that blue shirt disrespected them in their area because blue was the color of their rival gang, *the crypts*. My cousin told me if I would have gone to the corner, *I might not be alive today to write this story*. He said that they would have made an example of my ignorance. They would have shot me and left me lying there with a red bandana on my chest. They would have done it because I disrespected them by wearing the blue shirt on their turf. I quickly changed my shirt and as a matter of fact, I think I got rid of all of the blue and red tee shirts in my bags.

The word of God tells us to **be kind to strangers because we maybe entertaining angels unaware, Hebrew 13:2,** unknown to me the Lord sent an angel to assist me if only for a few blocks. I needed to reach a certain point that day and without that help I might not be here today. You may have a story of an encounter with an angel; he or she may have been a person on the street asking for alms to delay you for just a moment from crossing that street and being distracted for a moment, or the car that was meant for you, passed without any harm to you, because you stopped and helped him, or a little lonely old lady sitting on a park bench starts a conversation, you are busy but you took time to talk to her for a few moments and that bullet that was meant for you missed you. God knows the path we all take and He knows the plans He has for us. He uses His angelic host to help the ones He loves. He loves you, even when you don't think so. He keeps us from dangers seen and unseen. *Have you seen an angel lately?*

NOTES

HOW DO YOU FEEL ABOUT THIS STORY

CHAPTER 21

FAITH AND HEALING

THAT NIGHT MY AUNT CAME home from work tired but glad to see me. I told her that I was on my way home but could not make it the rest of the way. I told her that I needed to see a doctor. She told me about a hospital that was *free of charge*. I could have debated with her about the quality of health care in a free hospital. I could have questioned the type of doctors that would work for a free hospital, (those who could not make it in the mainstream hospitals). I felt they were the *C and D students* from medical school. I could have debated her about all of that... at that point, but I didn't. I would have gone for anything at that point because I needed some help. We arrived at the hospital in a cab and it was a long ride. I was lying on my stomach across the back seat all the way there. When I arrived at the hospital and approached the counter to sign in, the lady asked me what was the problem. I told her and she told me to fill out some forms and then to have a seat, boy, that was a card! *Have a seat?* I didn't know if she was trying to be funny or not. I stood by my aunt as she sat down in the only chair available. This place was a mad house. Tired from a long day's work, my aunt was able to sit down because someone got up – *"move your feet lose your seat,"* she grabbed that chair quickly, you know you got to be fast in the free hospital. I have never seen anything like that before, but that was what I should have expected from a free hospital. *Wall to wall sick people.*

I waited for about 10 minutes and the nurse called my name. She told me to go upstairs. There were people who were waiting longer than I, who started to complain. They wanted to know who I was and how was it that I could arrive after them and be allowed to see the doctor before them. *I just kept walking.* Upstairs was a larger room with a bunch of sheets used as dividers. The nurse told me to go into one of the spaces. I did. As I stood there, I heard the doctors talking and they said that one of the men up there had hepatitis. They discussed the space that he was in and it was right next to me. This man was coughing and gagging up a storm. I prayed, *"Lord, I don't want to die here."* The doctor came in, reading my chart and told me to bend over onto this contraption. It looked like a prayer altar found in church. I put my knees on the padded area and my arms over the top part of the device. My butt was sticking up in the air because I had to change into a gown. The doctor said that he would check the cysts to see if roots had grown. So, he did the same thing that the other doctor in Mississippi did. I thought it was a *conspiracy*, as he stuck those fingers up my behind without any consideration of my pain, needless to say, *that hurt*. The doctor then left and the nurse left as well. I was all alone except the man next to me; coughing uncontrollably. Kneeling down, with my butt in the air, I was exposed to everyone walking by and that was embarrassing. The man next to me kept on coughing, I said to myself, *"if the doctors don't kill me, the hepatitis would get me for sure!"* You may be laughing, but at that time, it was no laughing matter, *I was serious.*

After about 20 minutes, the nurse returned and asked, *'how was I feeling?'* She told me that the doctor would be right back, but first she would have to numb the area of my butt where the infection was located, because the doctor was going to singe the cyst. You must understand where this thing was. It was right in the crack of my rump. I was told that these things form because of the moisture in the area. The nurse told me to bend back over and to grab the handles on both sides of table where my arms were. I did as I was instructed; and she said not to look back and that it would pinch a little. *Of course, I looked back* and it was a good thing that I did because this lady had the largest syringe that I have ever seen in my life! It looked like something from a Dr. Suess book! I asked her, *"what in the world are you about to do with that thing?"* She said, *"I'm going to numb the area so that the doctor can singe the cyst. It would be too painful to endure if I don't numb you."* She then said that it wouldn't hurt, (*she lied*). *"Grab the post and hold on,"* she said. And, I did. I thought she was going to stick the needle in the side of my butt, but this woman stuck that needle right down the center of the cyst. I yelled loudly and almost jumped off of the stand. The nurse had the audacity to tell me to calm down. I told her, *"you calm down; you are not the one who just got stuck!"* Not only did she stick me, she moved the needle around in there and I felt myself passing out. She said, *"don't you faint on me!*" The doctor returned about five minutes later and took a scalpel and cut the thing to relieve the pressure. He told me that it was the puss that was causing the pain. After being numbed, I didn't feel anything the doctor did except the pressure of the scalpel. Then, the doctor told me that I had to sign some papers and that they had to give me something to take home with me. I returned downstairs and could barely walk. *I saw my aunt and she started to laugh. I asked her what was so funny and she said they all heard me scream upstairs and everyone knew that it was me.*

I stayed in Chicago for a couple of days until my Mom and Dad drove to Chicago and picked me up on the weekend after Dad got off of work.

After returning to Buffalo, I went to the doctor at ECMC. The doctor said that I needed surgery. The doctor also advised me that I had double hernias and that he would take care of those after I recuperated from the first surgery. I told him the Lord would heal me. He again stated that I should return to him after I recuperated from the first surgery. The night I came home after the surgery, I was sitting down on one of those blow up donuts and the telephone rang, it was my mother who was in church that night; there were some Evangelists in our church and the one that was preaching that night, asked was there an *Andre'* in the church. No one stood up, so she asked, *if anyone knew of an Andre' who just had surgery and the doctors told him that he needed another surgery.* Well, the Lord... could she had been more specific than that?! My Mom, if she had any doubts before, she had none now. Mom stood up and said that I was home recovering. The Sister Evangelist told Mom to call me and tell me that the Lord said that "*if I began to praise him and jump up, the Lord would heal my body and I would not have to have that second surgery,*" so she pass that bit of information on to me.

I remind you, now, I had just come home from the hospital earlier that day and was in no shape or mood to jump up and down. I considered the message I received. I questioned why would the Lord not heal me before the first surgery and to be honest, I was in so much pain, I wanted to just sit there, but I got up because I knew that this Sister Evangelist had heard from the Lord. I have seen what the Lord has done through her life's ministry and I knew she was giving a word of knowledge from God, because she didn't know of my situation. So, while in great pain, I slowly raised myself up and started to dance very carefully on my tippy toes; then I sat back down on my doughnut. It was a sight to see; good thing I was left there alone. It was a few days later, that I returned to the doctor for my check up and the doctor told me that I looked good and strong. *"Anytime you are ready to have the other surgery, come and see me,"* he said. I told him that God had healed me and I requested for him to check; the doctor checked once and he checked twice, then he looked confused at the x-rays that had showed the two tears in my testicle sack. The doctor said, *"I don't believe it!"* He did not see the tears, any longer, in my testicle sack! He then left the room and when he returned he was not alone; there was several people with him. They too, looked at the x-rays and *looked at me* and asked me if these are my x-rays. I responded, *"Yes."* Several of them came over and asked if they could check me out; reluctantly I consented to it. They looked at the x-rays and said there is no sign of any hernia, and that *there is a God of miracles*, the doctor said. I believe that God honored my faith and also wanted to prove to this doctor that *He is healer* and *He is God Almighty.* God made that doctor a believer. I hope from that experience; the doctor gave his life to the Lord. I asked a question, *'Why God didn't heal me from the first surgery?'* I believe that at the time of the first surgery, my faith was weak to believe for my healing. I believe that God needs our faith to partner with His word and then miracles happen!

A few months after, leaving Mississippi and my recovery, I sought out my biological father. I knew that he still lived in Buffalo and I just had to find him. I called my Aunt, *my father's sister.* I wanted to know if she had his address. She did and I went over to his house. When I arrived, no one was there but his *wife to be*; so I waited on him to come home. He finally came home and was surprised to see me. He hugged me and told me that it was a pleasure to see me. He looked me over and introduced me to his girlfriend; wife to be. They had three children and I met my little sister and brothers. That night I told him that I went to see my mother in Mississippi and had stayed with her for some time to get to know her and the girls. The reason that I visited him was because I wanted to stay with him to get a feel for who he was and wanted to get to know him better. He and his wife to be agreed to this. Things were not what I expected, though. I guess I really didn't know what to expect. I think I just wanted to spend time with him and to get a *sense of closure*. The time spent with him was eventful to say the least. The woman he lived with didn't get along with me, so well, though. Maybe, it was because I reminded her of my mother. So, I was there for about one week and moved out. I was still angry and now more disappointed than ever. I was hoping that this would fill in the gaps of my life, but all it did was bring further *confusion and anger.*

NOTES

HOW DO YOU FEEL ABOUT THIS STORY

CHAPTER 22

FAVOR AIN'T FAIR

I HAD A FRIEND NAMED Barry, who was a good man. One day, Barry asked me to go with him to his lady friend's house. I went with him and while I was there, I was introduced to a young lady who was the sister of his friend. My first glance at this young lady had me "*in there.*" We began dating at the disapproval of her mother. Her mother was a funny lady, she would tell me, "*I know what all men want with young girls.*" She wouldn't hold her tongue. She said what she felt and what she saw. I was really messed up at the time, still trying to prove my manhood. I wanted what I wanted and was determined to get it. *I pushed and pushed.* I told the young lady's mother that that was not my intentions… that I was saved, a man of God and went to church. I would even go with them to church to prove my holiness. You see, I was willing to do anything to get this girl and to win her mother over to trust me. I was not doing this to deceive her, I just didn't know how messed up I really was. One day, we had sexual intercourse and later on she notified me that she missed her monthly cycle. She was scared. I assured her that it was all right and that sometimes women missed their cycles, as if I was some authority on this issue. She went to the doctor and took a pregnancy test, sure enough the test turned out positive.

We told her mother and her mother cried; her mother did all she could do to prevent this, but I entered her life and now this. At that time, I didn't understand how her mother felt and still cannot fully understand. Now, having two daughters of my own, I can sort of feel how she must have felt. After all that time of protecting her daughter, it was all lost. I told her mother that I loved the young lady and her mother told me that I didn't know what *love* was. I got mad at her and said that I did. I thought, "*Who is this old lady, telling me that I don't know what love is?*" That old lady knew more than I thought she did.

So many times, in our lives, we are spoken to in wisdom, but we do not hear; our anger and bitterness and past experiences often causes us to be blind and deaf to the truth.

After finding out of the pregnancy, I felt ashamed and felt that it was entirely my fault. I blamed myself for messing up this young lady's life. She was on her way to college to be a nurse and I messed all that up for her. I told my parents about the baby and my dad told me to do the right thing, to take responsibility and be there for the child. He said, *"you made this bed now lie down in it."* I was not really aware of what those words fully meant, but I was soon to find out. Those words rang in me like a church bell tower and I was right next to the gong. Later that night, we attended church. I spoke to the pastor and told him what had happened. Because I was not married, the pastor was sorry to hear this and told me that I had to sit down from playing the drums for the church. I was the drummer at church and I was saved, *'so how did I get myself in that situation?'* It was not hard to get into that position because my flesh was not submitted to God's perfect will for my life and for my body. I get more into this in my next book entitled *"Just Like My Father."* In that book, I will talk about why I did the things that I did.

Finally, I had a little boy and we named him, *Andrew*. He was a handsome son. I vowed to be there for him at all cost *and I was*. The name *Andrew is Spanish for Andre'*. Many people asked, *'why didn't I make him a junior?'* At that time, I told them that I wanted him to have his own identity. Life got really difficult after my son was born. Things were good for a while, but the relationship changed with Andrew's mother and I. It seemed as if she was pushing me away. I tried my best to be there, but it was not good enough. She began seeing other people and that hurt… *mind you*, I was not a saint neither, but I didn't want this to separate us. I thought if I would buy her things and do things for her that maybe that would help us. I wanted to be there for my son and for his mother. I felt that if I wasn't there for them, I was not being a man and not standing up for my responsibilities. This had me bound, you see. I looked at many other relationships and saw the men who had babies and didn't stay with the mothers of their children; *chief of them was my biological father*. I said that I would not leave this girl. Because of that, I didn't want to be like other *dead-beat* fathers. I was taught better than that. *Truthfully, I didn't want to be like my biological father* and I didn't want to do what he did to me; left me and allowed me to be put up for adoption without ever fighting for me.

One day, some friends of mine told me about the police exam, that was coming up and asked if I was going to take the exam. I told them that I thought I would take it. Later that day, I talked to my dad (Scottie, as most of his friends called him.) I'll call him Scottie so that you will not get confused as to which dad I'm talking about. Scottie told me that if this is what I wanted to do, then go for it. What did I have to lose? At that time, I was working for Tops Supermarket, stocking shelves from 12:00 midnight to 8:30 a.m. *What did I have to lose?* Later, I heard about the qualifications necessary to qualify to be chosen to enter the Police Academy. All I had was a GED, not a high school diploma and no college degree, '*who was I kidding?*' I put the thought out of my mind and continued stocking shelves.

The deadline was approaching for the police exam and I don't even know why I went and got an application. I filled it out and took it to City Hall. I had it stamped and paid my application fee. I did it. The application was in and that was that. I also decided to take the fireman's exam, the State Troopers exam and the State Corrections exam. I received a notice to take the Police Officer's exam 9:00 a.m. on a Saturday. I had to work that Friday night at Tops. I left work and went straight to the place where the exam was given. There were thousands of men and women there waiting for the same opportunity to become a Buffalo Police Officer. We got in and sat down and was handed our tests. We were told to begin. I put my name on the test form and began to write. I may have gotten through twenty questions before I blanked out from exhaustion. When I finally awoke, I had only thirty minutes to complete the exam. No one around me would bother to wake me up. I guess they felt that I was just one less person that they had to compete with. I filled in the answer sheet without reading the questions, just filled them in.

Afterwards, I didn't think about that job because I knew I failed the test. I heard from the Correctional Department and decided to travel to Albany. After going through the grueling test they gave, I thought about the being locked up in jail and I decided this was not the job for me.

I later heard from the State Troopers and was asked if I wanted a job. I said, *"No,"* because I heard that you would be sent Upstate and I didn't want to leave my son. *I still kick myself for that one!* The Fire Department sent me the results of the test in the mail. I opened the mail and was very surprised to learn that I failed that exam. I could not believe that I failed it because that was the one, I felt that I had passed. It was so easy and I had great confidence. *That was a big blow to my pride.*

I found out that I had passed the police exam *with a great score.* I was as surprised as anyone. Again, not realizing the favor of God working.

Psalms 90:17

Let the favor of the Lord our God be upon us, and establish the work of our hands upon us; yes, establish the work of our hands!

NOTES

HOW DO YOU FEEL ABOUT THIS STORY

CHAPTER 23

KEPT

I WAS WORKING AT S&E Wholesale. It was an appliance store. They also sold some jewelry. I was the delivery person, along with an older gentleman named Ray, who knew a lot about delivery. I didn't agree with him on everything, but he was knowledgeable. At that time in my life, my son was the most important thing to me. Things were getting very hard. The money just wasn't there. Let me put it this way, I gave the money away. Trying to keep my responsibilities and the family happy, at the same time, drained me financially and spiritually. I had made the decision that I was going to take care of my son, *by any means necessary.* That decision cost me a lot; although, today, *I have no regrets.*

I stole some things from the store where I was working. I sold the items to have some extra money. One day, it was noticed that these items were missing. My employers asked me had I seen them and I said *"no"* just as easy as I did when my mother asked me about the $5.00 that was missing from her purse. The owner said that he wanted the items back and if he didn't get them, he was going to have everyone take a lie detector test. No one confessed, surely not me. Two days later, I arrived at work and the owner; said that I had to take a lie detector test. He took me and the other employees to take the test. When my turn came, I was not sweating at all. They plugged me up to the machine and asked me questions. Of course, I did not tell the truth. *I passed the test*! This is why these types of tests are not admissible in the courts. People can lie and pass these tests. Everyone passed the test and the Owner said, *"that's impossible, someone took the stuff."*

Months later, the Owner and I talked about God and the Bible. You see, he was a God fearing man; a good man and I stole from that man. There is a saying, ***"HURT PEOPLE HURT PEOPLE,"*** and not always because they want to hurt people, but out of their own dysfunction. One day, when I couldn't take it any more, I told the Owner that I took the stuff and that I was very sorry. He was hurt to hear that it was I, but was also relieved, too. The owner told me that he wouldn't fire me, although he had grounds to do so. He told me that he would trust me and give me another chance because he saw a good man in me. He understood that people do stupid things sometimes and that we all needed a second chance in life.

I continued to work there and had to make restitution for the stolen items. Every week, the owner took some money from my paycheck until I paid off the value of the stolen items. This was a crucial time in my life. *Here was a man that I stole from, but he gave me another chance. As I look back on that, I saw that God was in the mix.* If it had not been for this man of God, I probably would have gone to prison and had this theft on my record. During this time, I put my two weeks' notice in to my employer to prepare for the police academy, as I stated in a previous chapter I was let down by the Buffalo Police Department, after that I continued to check with the Police Academy to see what my status was. Once again, I was told that someone else knocked me off the list again. I was so angry. I just forgot about the Police Department! One day in January of 1989, I received a letter from the Buffalo Police Department asking me if I was still interested in the job. I couldn't believe it. *I really was going to be a Police Officer!*

The Police Academy was not easy at all. I had a hard time. Many things were going on at that time and I was going through many changes, my concentration was gone and truly the hand of God kept me through the Academy. I wanted to leave so many times, just as always, but for some reason, I stuck it out. *I didn't give up.*

Graduation time was approaching and I was happy that it was all over. Everyone was at the graduation and the Mayor of Buffalo was congratulating us. He spoke and said, *"some of you should not be here, but*

because of the Judge's ruling, you are here… so be thankful." That statement
set something off in all of the minorities in that room. I felt as though
I wanted to shoot the Mayor for such a statement. We all knew that he
was a racist and he didn't hold his words. He would let people know
that he didn't like them and was not ashamed of that. They still elected
him Mayor of Buffalo, *time and time again.* But for him to make such
a statement at our graduation was the lowest. We were all under his
leadership, too. *Ha, what a joke!*

I was later sent to Precinct #12, which I called the precinct in *East
Beirut.* That was because it was in a *war zone.* Drugs and homicide
were running rampant in this area. *The crime was so high and the life
expectancy; so low… there was not much hope that rang in the air.* This was
my assignment, I had to deal with it. I moved on Sobieski Street, not far
from the station house. My sister lived there and wanted to move out. I
took her apartment because the rent was cheap. That was a blessing for
me because I didn't have too far to go to work, only a one-block walk.

While at the Academy, I bought a little car from a place on Bailey
Avenue. It was a 1988 Skylark, white with blue interior. It was pretty.
That car cost me $5,000.00. I drove it for about three months; when the
engine caught on fire. I took the car back to the dealer and left it on the
lot. I told them to fix the car. They refused and said that I didn't put oil
in the engine and that was why it caught on fire. I didn't take the car
back, so they repossessed it. I was told that I owed the finance company
$5,000.00, plus attorney's fees. I was outraged, *to put it nicely.* I took the
dealer to Small Claims Court twice and won both times. Because the
dealer could switch names on the ownership of the company, I never
got any money. I was then forced to pay the Finance Company their
money. I was very upset, as anyone would be. All kinds of thoughts ran
through my mind. I could set the building on fire and stick rags in the
gas tanks and light them. *I'm being honest, these were my thoughts, but of
course, I did not do those things. I sure thought about doing them, though.
It was just a passing thought. Now don't act like you have never thought to
get back at someone before! You didn't follow through, but you sure thought
about it. Even if you would not have done anything yourself, you would have
applauded if someone else did.*

Those kinds of thoughts get people in trouble. Revenge is one bad dude. *"Because they did it to me, I'll get them back so help me God."* We even have nerve to put God in it, *as if He would help us to do wrong*! The Bible says, ***"Vengeance is mine said the Lord."*** The Lord said that He would repay those who do wrong. ***"The battle is not ours, but the Lord's."*** **Romans 12:19** sometimes we take things into our own hands and make a mess of things.

I was now walking to work because my car was gone. One day in December of 1989, my partner (*Dale was his name and he was a good cop*) and I were driving down Genesee Street on our way back to the station. We noticed a man banging on a window on the lower West Side of a house. We didn't pay much attention to him at the time. When we arrived at the station, we got a radio call on our car to go to a fire, at about the same address, where we saw this man hitting the window. We jumped back into the vehicle and got to the address and saw that the house was fully engulfed in flames. The man we saw earlier was screaming at us, telling us that his children were upstairs in the fire. At that time, other patrol cars came to assist us. The man ran upstairs into the upper apartment, which was full of flames. Without thinking, Dale and I, ran after the man. When we approached the top of the stairs leading to the apartment, the smoke was thick as pea soup and the heat was tremendous. We had to get on our hands and knees and crawl around. As I felt around me, I felt a leg in the smoky hallway. It was the leg of the man who ran in. He never made it into the house, he was overcome by smoke. Dale and I, pulled the man and others came in and carried him down the stairs. We could hear the kids screaming and crying for help. We tried to go into the apartment, but the heat was so great. The fire blew out the door as we attempted to enter again. The fire forced us down the stairs. We tried again and there was silence. We heard no more screams. *We had failed*! The firemen finally arrived and we rushed them into the house and told them where the screams were coming from. They sent us downstairs. All of the hair on my face had been burned from the heat in that place. Minutes went by and finally a fireman came from the building. In his arms was a little girl about two or three years old. She was limp and just lay dead in the fireman's arms. The fireman rushed to the ambulance and I began to cry at that sight. I thought of my own son who was about the same age as that little girl. The parents were crying. The father had to be strapped down to a bed because he was hysterical. He was still trying to get back to the fire yelling, "s*ave my children, save my children*." I looked up to heaven and prayed to God and asked Him to spare the lives of those children. With all that was in me, I cried out to God. I told everyone there to pray. I didn't care who they were. All I knew is that we needed to call on God on that day!

Another fireman came out of the fire and had another child in his arms. A third fireman came out with the last child and they were all in the same state as that first child. They lay limp over the arms of the firemen. People all around were in tears. You could have felt the heaviness of our hearts. We heard over the radio from the ambulance driver who had taken the first child to the hospital. They said that they had revived the child and was taking her into the hospital and notified the hospital to be ready. There was such a sense of hope there. But, that was not what I asked God to do. I told the Lord that there were two more children. Why I had such faith at that time, I do not know. I do know that I was very serious.

The other ambulances left and I was there waiting on God. Over the radio, I heard that they revived one of the twins on the way to the hospital. There was great rejoicing there. I looked to heaven and thanked God, but that was not what I asked God for. I asked for *all* of their little souls to be safe. I kept walking around and praying and after about ten minutes, we heard that the last baby was breathing and was going to be all right. I began to shout *"thank you Lord, thank you Lord"* at the top of my breath. I didn't care who heard me. I ran into a house where I knew the mother was and told her the news. She began to scream *"thank you Lord, thank you Lord."* She looked at me and said, *"thank you for believing."* Some may say that was neither the place nor the time for such a display of gratitude towards God. Not on the job. I don't care. *God answered my prayer.* Do you think that when Jesus healed the blind man in Matthew or the lame man in Luke that they waited til they got home to say *"thank you, Jesus… Glory to God!"* No, I don't think so! God showed me His miracle-working hand that day.

A month later, a letter came to the station house addressed to Officer Dale, thanking him for what he had done at the fire and said that the children were all doing fine. They only suffered some smoke inhalation in their lungs but were not burned. I pray, today, that their lives are blessed and that they are serving God, because God spared their lives *that day*. I believe He has a great purpose for each one of them.

As a Police Officer, just fresh to the force, you don't have a partner *per se*; you go with whomever the Lieutenant's put you with. There are times when you may be riding with someone that just left the Academy with you and neither of you know what you are doing. Sure, you may have the book knowledge, but not the street knowledge. Sometimes, senior officers do not want to ride with rookies. They want to ride with their partners. If the CO goes along with this game, then it is allowed to take place. This is dangerous for the rookies because there is not always someone out there to help you make the right decisions. That can cost someone his or her life. People do not know how scary it is to come out of the academy and fresh on the streets and thrown into the den of lions on the mean streets. *Every moment at any moment could mean life or death.*

I had several partners in Precinct #12 at the Genesee Street Station. They were good men and women who upheld the law. One day, I was assigned to ride with a lady officer, named Sharon and this officer had been on the precinct for a few years and was good at her job. We got a call on Box Avenue that a lady was having problems with her son. Upon arrival, we were let into the home and there was the son sitting in a chair and his mother was sitting on the couch. The mother told us of the problem and stated that the son just started attacking her. The mother told her son that he would have to leave because she was not going to stand for disrespect in her own house. That's when the son pushed his mother and smacked her. He told her that he was going nowhere. Suddenly, this boy jumped up and started to swear at his mother. He began to call her out of her name. Sharon told him to sit down and to calm down. Of course, he refused. Sharon told him once again to sit down and stop swearing and to show some respect. Boy, that set him off. He got into Sharon's face and that's when I began to move closer to them. He wouldn't back up, so Sharon pushed him out of her face and he went berserk. He put his hand on Sharon's face and tried to push her back. I grabbed him and threw him into the chair. He tried to stand and was cursing Sharon out and asking her who she thought she was. At that point, he started swinging and before I knew it, out came Sharon's baton and *POW!* It hit that boy right in the forehead. I don't think that was where she wanted it to land, but that's where it landed. He stumbled back into the chair, still swearing. Just as swiftly as Sharon swung that baton, there was a golf ball sized knot on his forehead. The mother was in a rage! *"Don't hurt him, he's a good boy... Don't hurt him!"* This <u>boy</u> was about 30 years old. I left that house very disturbed and confused. We went there to help this mother because she called us, but she was defending," the boy" as she called him. I was not sure if this was a mother's natural love for her son, in spite of him putting his hands on her and swearing at her or plain blindness and deafness? I road with Sharon several times after that and we seemed not to get along too well. I felt she was too bossy. I felt that way because she had more seniority *over me*; and she was letting me know it. When we went out on calls, she would do all the talking and I would do all the writing. That made it look like she had me under control; especially to the people we had to deal with. I walked the beat also and that was a lonesome assignment, I *often walked alone.*

I was transferred to Precinct #7, (a very slow place). Not much went on down there. Mostly plants and abandoned buildings. The most excitement was watching the rats the sizes of raccoons try to make it across the road without getting hit. Grain Mills were over in that area and the rats got all they could eat, at any time. One night, I was in the car and the radio gave a call to assist a person with a drunken man in her hallway. The man refused to move. My partner and I arrived and another car came to assist. We went to the door and tried to enter. There was a man on the floor in the lower hallway, so the officers couldn't get in. We tried to push the door open to gain entry, but the man kicked the door and it struck one of the officers who had his arm in the door. They went crazy trying to push the door open. It was dark and the man started kicking and officers started hitting. The man started bleeding and I was still outside. After the man was cuffed and put into the police car, one of the officers asked me why didn't I go into the hall to help them out? I told him that there were enough people in the hallway. There were five of them in there and no one else could fit. Afterwards, they told the Captain, at the time they didn't want to work with me, because I was dangerous and would not help if the need arose. The Captain put me on days. That was the best thing that happened to me. *Rookies didn't even think about days, much less go on days. They thought this was hurting me, but it was a blessing in disguise.*

One day in the summer of 1990, while on routine patrol, I was riding with a gentleman named Will. He was a funny man, as we left the station house, we were stopped by a car full of men screaming at us, telling us that their friend was just shot by some men who were running through the Perry Projects. We went after them. Will drove the car down South Park Avenue and stopped. We saw the man that was described by the men in the car. We took chase and as we were running, we split up to cut the man off. As we did this, we came back together at the end of the building. All of a sudden, one of the men's arms came out with a gun. *He fired a shot at us!* Boy, was I surprised. I saw Will hit the ground out of the side of my eye and I thought he had been hit. Instant fear gripped me like a vice grip. I started towards Will and he returned fire. I screamed, *"Are you hit?"* He said no and then I began to return fire. There I was… *'a rookie in a shootout.'* While in the Academy, we met men who told us that during the 20 years as police officers, they never had to pull out their guns, nor less shoot them. We all believed that would be the case for us. *It was not true in my case.* While we were shooting at the men, a car came out of nowhere with an elderly couple in it. They were right in front of our line of fire, so we had to stop firing to prevent these people from being injured. The shooters were fleeing and there were other patrol cars coming. We kept chasing them and finally we caught them along with the help of other officers. It's funny how your mind can play games with you. My chest began to hurt and I thought I was shot, so I pulled at my shirt and vest saying, *"I'm hit, I'm hit!"* I felt blood running down my chest. Finally, as others came to help me get my clothes off, *I realized that I was not shot at all; but that sweat ran down my chest.* The pain in my chest was simply because I was out of shape. *You may be laughing, but at that time, it was not funny*!

André A. Scott

Isaiah 54:17 NKJ

No weapon formed against you shall prosper, And every tongue which raises against you in judgment You shall condemn.

God will keep you, no matter where you may find yourself, the weapon may be formed, but God says it will not prosper, God says that He created the black smith who formed the weapon, so God knows that it has no ability to take you out.

Well, I just told you a little about my life and the events that surrounded it. I will tell more, at a later time, *in another book*. Although it appears I had a normal life, I didn't tell you what I was dealing with at that time. All of the insecurities that I dealt with came from being abandoned. I was so bitter during these times, that *I didn't know which way was up. Although it may seem that I was in control, I was totally out of control. Because I always felt abandoned as a child, this played into my life like a bad horror story.*

NOTES

HOW DO YOU FEEL ABOUT THIS STORY

_____

_____

_____

_____

_____

_____

_____

_____

_____

_____

_____

_____

_____

_____

_____

_____

_____

_____

_____

_____

_____

_____

_____

CHAPTER 24

ANGELS WATCHING OVER ME

I ENDED THE CHAPTER ON "*help is on the way,*" with talking about the little boy who carried my suitcase; let me talk about him for a moment.

I thought nothing of it at the time, but many years later, I was teaching a class in *Bible School on Angelology.* We were discussing the scripture, "**be careful how you treat strangers, for you may be entertaining angels unaware.**" **(Hebrew 13:2)**. The question to the students was, "*have you seen an angel?*"

I began thinking about that day and I realized something strange about that young boy... *He just appeared.* I don't know where he came from. I looked around and there was no place for him *to come from;* there was no driveway, there was no stores opened, there was no building for him to come out of... *he just appeared.* That day, as I turned to pay him $5 for carrying my suitcase, he was gone just as quickly as he appeared; he awesomely disappeared.

I thought heavily about what happened in Chicago that day and how the boy *appeared and disappeared.* The spirit let me know that *that* was *my angel* to help me that day, to get within eye shot of *my cousin.* If it had not been for my help; I would have missed my encounter with Hakeem and could have lost my life that day. Further, my cousin was my angel, as well; I did not realize, I was in gang territory, so no matter what, always remember that... **Help was on the way.**

Another encounter with angels, was while in junior high school, I was a student at school #44, which is now known as *Lincoln Academy.* I had some good times and there were some not-so-good times, and this particular morning, was one of those *not so good days.* I went to school in a predominately *white Polish immigrant* neighborhood. There were some polish people in that neighborhood who were very proud and ignorant. Many days on the way to school, we would get into fights with some of them who would shout at us and call us *nigger's* and tell us we were on polish ground and we're not welcome. *I am putting this nicely.*

The language that was used was very degrading to any race (ethnicity). Every day before school, whether rain or sunshine, several of the black and white guys would meet in the rear of the school building and play basketball, so I would usually get picked to play on the first team. (*I was a pretty good ball player, I thought I might throw that fact in, even though it has no bearing on the story!*)

This was pretty much the routine, but this day as the school bell rang, we began to leave the playground. Suddenly cars loaded with white drunken males pulled up and jumped out of their cars with bats, chains and knives and began chasing some of the black females. We heard the commotion and came to see what was happening. We engaged them and a fight ensued; this time, we were tired of running from these bullies, so that day we stood our ground. I got in a tussle with one of the guys… I had him on the ground and was wailing away on him. I got pushed off of him and got up, ready to go at it some more. I said, "*Come on, any one of you!*" Someone yelled, "DUCK," so I instinctively ducked and instantly after I lowered my body, there was a loud sound, I looked up and pieces of wood were flying around in the air. There was a guy standing there with a shattered bat in his hand. He dropped the bat and they all ran and got into their vehicles and drove off. The teachers came running outside to see what was happening, *a little late I might add*, (they should have been put into detention),. But, it all happened so fast, I did not pay much attention to what happened, but many years later, when I began to feel really depressed about the way my life was looking and angry at God for making me the way He did, being 5'8, ok 5'7 ½… *wanting to be at least 6' feet; the Lord let me know He made me perfectly and does not make mistakes*! If on that day I had been one inch taller, I would not be writing about this story today; He said, "*the bat would not have splintered but my head would have.*" "**I praise you because I am fearfully and wonderfully made.**" **(Psalms 139:14)**

God told me that He loved me and that He was there for me. He reminded me of that particular day, when I had that fight. He told me that it was my angel who spoke to me and I responded. He spared my life that day because He loved me and He had a purpose for my life! **There are Angels watching the over me!**

Let me tell one more angel encounter story. My Mom took myself and my younger siblings to the water park down at LaSalle Park, better known as *the Waterfront Park*; this day we were told not to go into the pool area, to only stay in the kiddy sprinkler play area, while Mom walked away momentarily, I got this bright rebellious ideal to do what I wanted to do, driven by my lustful male youth. I walked into the deep pool area, I was motivated after seeing the *pretty girls* clapping for the boys who were diving off the diving boards; I wanted to show off and be like them. I entered the area and stood in line to dive... my turn was *up* next and I wanted to show these girls, that I was somebody too. I climbed the stairs leading to the platform of the diving board, then walked out onto the board; my knees buckled from fear because I have never done this before; nor had I ever been on a diving board. I tried to imitate what I saw the other guys do, but I froze up there. I heard the boys say, *"come on jump."* I turned around to go back, but I saw the girls looking intensely at me and I got confidence (*smile*). I walked up and pushed off and did what is called a perfect swan dive. I hit the water with such grace and accuracy, *down, down, down,* I went into 12 feet of water. I touched the bottom and pushed off with my legs up. I went, *"wow,"* was that a rush, when suddenly I heard in my ear, *"fool you are going to die today!"* I immediately came to myself and realized that I could not swim. I panicked and began to kick and swing my arms, hysterically, in the water. As I began to take in water, I attempted to yell for help. I could see the *Lifeguards* sitting in their towers; but none came to assist. *So, down, down, down again I went.* While sinking to the depths of this pool, my life began to flash before me and I heard again, *"you are going to die"* as I reached the bottom... again, I pushed off with my legs and I felt okay this time. *"I'll get help,"* I remembered hearing someone say before that... *if you go down a third time you will drown.* I came to the surface, with no help, tired and very weak.

I gave into the words that I was going to die today down, down, down I went and with no strength to fight any more... all of a sudden the water in the pool was dispersed with bubbles, all around me. I saw two very large muscular men coming towards me; they had bronze looking bodies as if they had a perfect suntan, wearing red Speedos. They grabbed me and pulled me up to the surface next to the pool wall, where I was able to pull myself up out of the water. I set on the edge of the pool breathing deeply to catch my breath and with water in my eyes, *snot... okay mucus* running from my noise. I looked on both of my sides and there were some young ladies sitting beside me. I asked them, '*where did the Lifeguards go who pulled me from the water?'* No shame in my game at *this point*; but the girls looked at me strangely, as if there was something wrong with me, and one of them answered, "*no guard pulled you from the water you came out alone.*" I looked at the Lifeguard towers in disbelief and the guards who were sitting in their seats watching the pool. Now that's something to *praise the Lord* about, **He keeps us from dangers seen and unseen, even when we place our own selves in danger. He is faithful to watch over us.**

I know that there are many reading this right now, whose life may be similar to my story... it may even mirror mine, in certain aspects... I would like to tell you that God is on your side and there are **ANGELS** watching over you to keep you, too! I know it doesn't look like it right now, it looks real dark and as if there is no way out, but I tell you that God has a way of escape. *"There is no temptation that has taken you; such as common to man, but God, who is faithful, will not allow you to be tempted, above that which ye are able; but with the same temptation, make a way of escape, that ye may be able to bear it." (1 Corinthians 10:13)*

NOTES

HOW DO YOU FEEL ABOUT THIS STORY

CHAPTER 25

~~~

MANY FATHERS

THERE COULD BE TIMES IN our lives, where we may feel that no one loves or cares about us; for my teenage years and most of my adult life, I was there and I felt that I didn't give any one a reason to love me, so I tried to find it in all the wrong places. You know that same old story… *the devil has been tricking 'man' for a very long time.*

Growing up was hard for me; *so many feelings, so many problems, so many issues.* Every one of us has issues in our lives… some are deeper than others. They may be different but *they all hurt.* Because I didn't deal with my anger or bitterness appropriately, I found myself in bad situations. Many people would tell me, that I thought I knew everything, and I would deny acting like that. I tried to make myself fit in every conversation. I had to have something to say; even if they weren't taking to me or asked my opinion, I'd just *butt in.* I guess that wouldn't have been so bad, if at least some of the time, I was right. *I became this way because people would tell me that I was stupid and I would never amount to anything in life.* "**Don't believe the 'Naysayers'!**"

Today, now that I have allowed Father God to heal me… I don't have to know everything, nor prove my worth and value to anyone. I even found out that I don't even have to prove myself to Father God for Him to love me. I'll talk more about the "Fathers Love," in my next book entitled *"Just Like My Father."* (Stay tuned). Now, I call myself the *good son*; no longer the *bad son.* Since the Lord has changed my life, I have so many father's and mother's that I laugh, because every were I go… I pick up a new set of parents! Once I felt I had none, now I have an abundance; *that's what He will do… Child of God*, he really knows how to fix you!

> *"Even if you had ten thousand guardians in Christ, you do not have many fathers, for in Christ Jesus I became your father through the gospel."* **1st Corinthians 4:15**

NOTES

HOW DO YOU FEEL ABOUT THIS STORY

_____

_____

_____

_____

_____

_____

_____

_____

_____

_____

_____

_____

_____

_____

_____

_____

_____

_____

_____

_____

_____

_____

_____

CHAPTER 26

THE CHOSEN SON

"For He chose us in Him before the creation of the world to be holy and blameless in His sight. In love he predestined us to be adopted as his sons through Jesus Christ, in accordance with his pleasure, to the praise of his glorious grace, which he has freely given us the One He, loves." (**Ephesians 1:4-6**).

THIS SCRIPTURE SHOULD CHANGE THE way you feel about *'Adoption.'* If you feel no one loves you or wants you; God is saying He does and that He chooses to have you to be a part of his glorious family, *(a son)*. It doesn't matter, if anyone loves you or takes you in, God will accept you just as you are. He wants you to come to him and be a part of His winning family; to be part of His glorious Kingdom. God has already predestined you to be His! He made a way that those who are not *His*; that they would become *His* through *His son Jesus Christ*. God is pleased to have you as His sons and daughters. So, lift up your head, stick out your chest and say *I'm a son.* A child of the King! *Praise the Lord*!

Did you know that Jesus the Christ was *"adopted?"*

After he considered this, the angel of the Lord appeared to him in a dream, *"Joseph son of David, do not be afraid to take Mary home as thy wife, because what is conceived in her is from the Holy Spirit. She will give birth to a son, and you are to give him the name Jesus, because he will save his people."* (**Matthew 1:18-24**).

Joseph was not the father of Jesus; the Holy Spirit implanted the God seed in Mary's womb and she conceived. Joseph and Mary did not have pre-marital relations. You see, Joseph *adopted* Jesus as his son.

If Jesus was *adopted* then *adoption* is a good thing. Jesus was *adopted* so that we also could be *adopted* into the body of Christ.

I grew up believing that *adoption* was the worst thing that could ever happen to a child; this was because of my pain and woundedness, as I blamed everything that went wrong in my life, *on being adopted*. I used this as my foundational excuse for not wanting to deal with my truth *and that truth was I needed to forgive my father and mother for abandoning me.*

> **"For you did not take the spirit of bondage again in fear, but to whom you took the Spirit of adoption as children we cry, Abba Father." (Romans 8:15).**

Adoption is one of the greatest gifts that a family or person can offer a child. *Adoption* says that I choose you. Wow! I choose you... *someone really chose me. Adoption is a choice;* whereby a family chooses to give you their name and add you to their family *as their own. Praise the Lord... I was chosen*!

Even more than the fact that, man chooses us to be a part of this earthly perishing family, God chooses us to be a part of his eternal family... NOW THAT'S GREAT NEWS!

NOTES

HOW DO YOU FEEL ABOUT THIS STORY

_____

_____

_____

_____

_____

_____

_____

_____

_____

_____

_____

_____

_____

_____

_____

_____

_____

_____

_____

_____

_____

_____

_____

_____

CHAPTER 27

I KNOW HOW YOU FEEL

WHAT'S FUNNY IS WHEN I was growing up and I would talk to people about how I felt about being adopted, I was trying to open up; they would say, "I know how you feel," *this really tee'd me off,* because they didn't know *how I felt.* They had no ideal about the pain I was in... they had not been there; nor had they been *fostered or adopted.* Sometimes I would tell them, *"you don't know,"* out of my anger. I was so full of hurt, that I would get angry. I could feel the volcano erupting in me. *I was so touchy* that people could trigger my emotions and not even know it.

The bible tells us, **"He was despised and rejected by men, a man of sorrows, and familiar with suffering. Like one from whom men hid their faces he was despised, and we esteemed him not. Surely, he took up our infinities and carried our sorrows, yet we considered him stricken by God, smitten by Him and afflicted, but He was pierced for our iniquities; the punishment that bought us peace was upon him, and by his wounds we are healed. We all like sheep has gone astray, each have turned to his own way; and the Lord laid on Him the iniquity of us all." (Isaiah 53:3-6).**

The Lord has been where you are now. The word says that he was *bruised for our iniquities* and because he took on himself all of our hurts and pains and have gone through this, *we can be healed.* Isn't that great to know... that he bore all this because he loved us *then,* and he loves us *now!* **"He's the same yesterday today and forever." (Hebrews 13:8) NIV.** No matter what it is, how bad it may seem to be; *He did it once and for all.* It's time for you to be healed. Let go of all that extra baggage that you have been carrying around for so long. You no longer need to hold on to bitterness, loneliness or the shame, because the Lord says, **"Come Unto me, all you who are weary and burdened, and I will give you rest. Take my yoke upon you and learn from me, for I am gentle and humble** *in heart, and you will find rest for your soul. For my yoke is easy and my burden is light."* **(Matthew 11:28-30) NIV.** The Lord wants your weights, your burdens; He wants to give you rest for your weary souls; you can find it in God today.

NOTES

HOW DO YOU FEEL ABOUT THIS STORY

_____

_____

_____

_____

_____

_____

_____

_____

_____

_____

_____

_____

_____

_____

_____

_____

_____

_____

_____

_____

_____

_____

_____

CHAPTER 28

FOR HIS GLORY

I FOUND OUT SOMETHING VERY powerful! And that is… What you have been going through is not just for you. Right now, you may feel hopeless in your attempts to break free from the bondages that have held you, and it seems as if you cannot go any further in life. STOP and LISTEN to what He's telling you right now. The word of God says, *"And we know that all things work together for the good to them that love God, and them who are the called according to his purpose. For whom he did foreknow, he also did predestinate to be conformed to the image of his son, that they, might be the firstborn among many brethren. Moreover, whom he did predestinate, them he also called and whom he called them he also justified and whom he justified them he also glorified. What shall we say to these things? If God before us who can be against us."* (**Rom. 8:28-31**).

It's like this, all that we've been through in our lives, God has a purpose for it. You may say '*why me?*' Because you have been predestinated to become his son. The sufferings that you have seen has been to make you better and to make you an example of how mighty He is. Apostle Paul puts it this way, *"I consider that our present sufferings are not worthy of comparing with the glory that is to be revealed in us."* (**Roman 8:18**).

It's not over! The end is not now… you don't have to "*check out.*" All you need is to allow the Lord to heal you and deliver you from captivity. The Lord told me that he was going to use the testimony of my life, to take me to where he had purposed; if I would only let go and let him do the work in me. *The road was already paved for my destiny.* I tell you… that no devil in hell can stop what God has for you, because "*what God has for you is for you!*" Don't surrender over to the devil anymore. Allow the Lord to shine his *purification light* on you, in you and through you… *this day*! Say, I surrender to God's will and purpose for my life. I forgive… I accept forgiveness and I forgive myself, therefore releasing me from the yokes of bondage and destroying the chains that bound me. God wants the glory out of our lives. What He's going to do in you and through you… you won't believe.

I'm prophesying now, because I feel the anointing of the Father, on me… even as I am writing, this for someone. Someone, like you! *Just as Evangelist Sharon, called me out*! Father God says, that he is doing a *new thing* in you. He's going to break the bondage off of your life and he's going to lift you up! ***"And I will restore to you the years that the locust hath eaten,"* (Joel 2:25a)** and he's going to cause you to forget your barrenness and cause you to forget the shame of your youth… *this is a new day!*

Lift up your hands and Praise the Lord! I pray to you… the Reader, now… that you, *like myself,* would be filled with joy and peace, (which surpasses all understanding) from this moment on and that you would use your God given testimony to bring much harvest and glory to His Kingdom, *Amen!*

> ***"Now the Lord of peace himself give you peace always by all means. The Lord be with you all."* (II Thessalonians 3:16)**

NOTES

HOW DO YOU FEEL ABOUT THIS STORY

_____

_____

_____

_____

_____

_____

_____

_____

_____

_____

_____

_____

_____

_____

_____

_____

_____

_____

_____

_____

_____

_____

_____

_____

CHAPTER 29

BLAME GAME

GROWING UP, I BLAMED ALL my troubles on being adopted, as I stated in my previous chapters. I hated my biological parents because I could not believe they would do this to me. How could they just leave me with someone else and not come back for me? I hated my father, but I was mad at my mother, more because I found out that she had two other children after she gave me up. As I *grew*, in the home of the Scott family, my anger was directed towards them. I didn't understand it at the time, but there is a saying that, *"you hurt the ones you love the most."* I found this to be true. When I was stealing from my mother, I didn't see it as stealing from her, but as only taking what I wanted. I found this was due, in part, to being adopted. *People who have been adopted often steal because they feel that some things were taken from them.* I would shut people out and not allow them in my life. I had put up a wall and push them away. This would hurt me many times, but I would not let anyone else know it. I was protecting myself at all costs. No one would be able to hurt me like my parents did.

That anger and bitterness was eating away at me to the point, that I was just a shell with *nothing inside*. I wouldn't hold a job for long and I could not keep my focus. If I didn't want to go to work, I wouldn't. I had no accountability and no stability. I wouldn't be committed to anything and would leave if I wanted to. I didn't trust anyone; basic trust was needed in my life but because I couldn't trust my biological parents, I figured everyone would do me the same way. They would leave. In order to protect myself, I would not let them in or trust them. I felt that I didn't belong, even when my family told me that I was loved, I still pushed them away. I was mean and sharp with my tongue. *The wall was UP and I would not let anyone in!* The sad part was that I was searching for love; *trying to get it.* Many people who never seem to feel that they fit in anywhere usually turn to drugs and a life of crime.

I was also *selfish* and that selfishness followed me even into my marriage and with my children. This affected them. We must understand that when we are in this state, it not only affects us but also those around us. I would buy candy and hide it in a drawer, so that I could eat it when I wanted it. One day, my daughter was rumbling through my desk and came across my stash. My wife found out about it and told me that it was wrong to hide food. I told her that it was because I wanted it to be there when I wanted it. I felt that it was okay for me to do this, but one day I asked a Christian psychiatrist about it and he told me that this was a *reflex* feeling that *I had to keep something to myself* and I had to have something to hold on to. Because something was missing from me, I felt that I had to keep some things for myself. *That's a problem.*

There are many ways that a person may react to *adoption* and you may not see yourself here. But, there is something that must be dealt with. I have talked with people who have been adopted and asked them what was the one thing that they seemed to have to deal with. They all said they always had a feeling that in a relationship, the person they were with would leave them. *This comes from that abandonment spirit.* This is not just for those who have been adopted, but also for those who have lost parents due to death, or divorce, (for those whose fathers walked out on them and their mothers at a young age). Even those whose mothers and fathers have left them, may have dealt with this type of experience. *This is a growing problem in our society today.* Abandonment issues is no game, *it is real.* It has broken up families; marriages and separated children from loved ones. It is also the cause of several suicides throughout our history. As a cop on the street, I could see the effects of this animal called, *abandonment.* After arresting certain people, I wondered what their home lives were like; so, I would ask them. *Some would not talk, but those who talked to me all fell into the categories of missing a father, a mother or fostered/ adopted.* Is there some correlation to those who do crimes? I say, unapologetically, YES! I went through it myself, but only by the grace of God, am I able to write this book as a *free man* both *spiritually and naturally.* I am not behind any prison doors, and that's a miracle in itself!

One day as I as working, I received a call on Coit Street. I am not sure what the call was about, but as we were over there, the mailman happened to be late and the people were outside waiting on him. It was check day and welfare checks and other support checks were expected. The people were quite upset because the mailman was late. One lady was walking towards us and telling one of her friends that she would kill the postman if the bank was closed when he arrived. She said she was upset that she wouldn't be able to cash her check that the foster agency was sending her, it was Friday night and she had to go buy herself a new dress to go out in… so she could party. She also needed cigarettes! This bothered me greatly because as she was walking down the street, running behind her were three little children whose clothing looked like they wore them for the past three weeks. They were dirty and worn out. The children looked as though they hadn't had baths in weeks. But this woman, her hair was *done* and she *looked okay*. She even had the senselessness to say that she had those kids so that she could get paid. She said that *the system* paid well. She told her friend, *"girl, you should get you some kids."* This grieved me so. I was brought up in a foster home with parents that never made me feel that I was any different than their own children. *Whatever they got, we got*. There was always food on the table, *every day* and *lots of it*. As a growing boy, I always had seconds. Our clothing was clean and ironed and our shoes always fit. We may not have had the *top of the line* sneakers, *but I had sneakers on my feet!*

I remember one day, when mom took us all to Liberty Shoe Store on Broadway and got each of us some sneakers. They were called *buddies*, but they were *new and I was proud of them*. As we got home, I went outside to show my new sneakers and some of my friends laughed at me because they said that my sneakers were *buddies*. They sang a song, *"you may slip and slide if you don't have the ones with the stars on the side."* That made me so mad so I said, *"We will see. I will race any one of you who said that these were buddies."* Boy, did I open my mouth or put my sneaker in it! Several of the boys stepped up and got in line to race me. Someone said, "go" and off we went. I reached the finish line first; *of course*. I was the fastest kid around in those days. I told the kids, *that the sneakers without the star on the side just beat their butts*! As I walked back down the street, to where the other kids were, I looked on the ground and saw parts of the sneakers on the pavement! Those sneakers melted on the pavement! There are times I totally forget that I was adopted. This is why it hurt me so much to have seen this woman dressed like she was and to see those kids dressed like they were. The woman was taking the money that was for the kids and using it for her selfish pleasures. It was all about the money, not to provide a stable home for these children.

That may be the case with someone reading this now, I don't know, but if this is… you may still have anger and bitterness, God wants to heal you and deliver you from this yoke of bondage.

> *"And it shall come to pass in that day, that his burden shall be taken away from off thy shoulder, and his yoke from off thy neck, and the yoke shall be destroyed, because of the anointing."* **(Isaiah 10:27)**

I thought that adoption was a curse and a bad thing, I felt this way because of my bitterness and wounded spirit. As I began to read the Word of God for myself; I found out that *I was a gift from God* and that I was loved by Him even if it was true that no one else loved me. He loved me more than I knew and He wanted me to know this. As I read the Bible, God showed me that Jesus was adopted. God impregnated Mary by the Holy Spirit and Joseph was not the natural father of Jesus, but he adopted the baby Jesus as his own. Everyone called Jesus the son of Joseph. Many successful and great people throughout history were adopted.

Some of you reading this are Christians and have been hurting for a long time, not knowing what to do. You sought the Lord and it seems that there is no hope that this is the way it is. You have lost all hope for deliverance, but God has this to say to you:

> **"Listen to me, you islands; hear this, you distant nations: before I was born the Lord called (knew) me; from my birth, he has made mention of my name, you are my servant in whom I will display my splendor."** **(Isaiah 49:1,3)**

In other words, God is saying that before your parents knew of you… *He knew you.* Before they thought of you; He knew you and already had a plan for your life and *it is a good plan.* He talked about you to His son, Jesus and the angels and plotted out your life. He called you His servant and said that you will show His greatness to men. Then he sent you from Himself and gave you as a gift to the world and placed in you gifts and talents for you to display for His glory. Don't look at other people's lives and how they turned out; but thank God for yours! We all have different beginnings and even the middle part is different, but the end can be the same. The Bible tells us that *the gift of God is eternal life*. Jesus is the gift to man and He has also given gifts to the world. So, pick up your head and stop dragging your feet and run to Jesus today… He will show you the way!

Let me leave you with this, it took a long time to come to this point in my life and it is not going to happen overnight, *it is a process. Trust God and trust the process and He will bring you through.*

Ask those who you hurt to forgive you, ask your parents whether you know them or not to forgive you for the bitterness you have held in your heart. Release them so that you can be released also. Then ask God to forgive you for being angry with Him for bringing you into this world.

I want to talk to the mothers and fathers, who have released their children into the lives of other people, for whatever the reason, if you are reading this… then God is speaking to you and He's saying, **He Loves you too**.

NOTES

HOW DO YOU FEEL ABOUT THIS STORY

_____

_____

_____

_____

_____

_____

_____

_____

_____

_____

_____

_____

_____

_____

_____

_____

_____

_____

_____

_____

_____

_____

_____

CHAPTER 30

THE FATHER'S LOVE

SEE THE DEVIL WANTS TO destroy you with the guilt and condemnation of what took place, but God tells us in His word, **"there is therefore, no condemnation for those who are in Christ Jesus." (Rom. 8: 1)**. I know that God can and will heal the hurts and the wounds and the empty feelings that you feel inside. The one thing that the Lord showed me was that a parent that gave their child up goes through their own private hell, because it was not an easy decision they made, but they must live with it. Most of the time, those foster children who judge their parents for this, need to understand and see the other side. The devil wants to bring you down through condemnation, but the Lord wants to build you up through His Love.

God loves you just as much as he loves the child you gave birth to. The Lord has a plan, and I found this out a while ago; that God knows what's going to happen before it happens and that He already made a way for your child, just like He made away for you. As the Lord takes me back over my life, I can see the hand of the Lord all over me; even when I was not thinking of God nor wanted to hear anything about God. He changed my mind and not only my mind but also this heart of mine. No longer do I belong to *myself*... but to the Lord. *God has a bright future in store for you, too.* I told my parents that I loved them and asked them to forgive me for judging them when I had no right to do so. I told them that I turned out all right and *for them* to thank the Lord *for not only saving me, but for healing me and keeping me.* If you are feeling condemned, ask God to forgive you and he will, then forgive yourself. Don't allow condemnation to hold you any longer.

Let me pray for you, *"Father in the name of Jesus, I know your power and I know that you are a deliverer... Father, I come on behalf of all those children whose parents have given them up. I stand in the gap for them and say to these parents that I forgive them for what took place and that I no longer hold it against them. I release them in the name of Jesus! Father, now heal the woundedness with in these parents; Lord wrap your arms around them and demonstrate your great love to them… that from this day forward their lives will never be the same again and that the purpose that you have for their lives will continue to prevail. Give them, Father, the fulfillment that belongs to them, that comes only from you."*

Now say this with me, *"Oh Lord, I accept your love for me and I thank you for this new lease on life; this new gift of life. I now forgive myself and I pray that I will no longer walk in condemnation ever again."*

Now give God some praise for what he has done and will do and kick the devil in the butt! You're an official, *"Kick the devil, in the butt, kind of a parent!"*

I blamed my parents for the things that went wrong in my life. I wasn't born with a silver spoon in my mouth nor did I come from a rich family and everything didn't go right for me as you can see; but I can say *thank God*. I can see the hand of God, on my life now, yet I didn't see it while going through it. Several times I thought about committing suicide and just ending it all. I had low self-esteem and I valued my life as worthless. I felt that no one loved me and I was in a self-destruct mode. The devil was there to help me get there fast; but, *"If it had not been for the Lord on my side, I don't know where I would be."*

Fathers and mothers, God loves you so much that, ***"He sent his only begotten Son, that whosoever believeth on him should not perish but have ever lasting life."*** **(John 3:16).**

NOTES

HOW DO YOU FEEL ABOUT THIS STORY

CHAPTER 31

WHAT I FEARED THE MOST

IN THE EARLIER CHAPTERS, I spoke regarding my relationship with my biological father, *even that sounds strange now*, but I'll use biological father for the purpose of this writing, in which I use it to identify which father I am referring to; but throughout my life, growing up, I hated my father and mother. I despised the thought of them bringing me into this world and for everything that went wrong, I blamed them for it and said, '*if they would have not given me up this would not have happened.*' I used them as *my* excuse for *all* my pain.

One evening, I was sitting in church when I heard a voice say, "*you must forgive your father.*" I looked behind me and there was no one within three to four rows; so, I shook it off and continued to enjoy the service. Then, I heard it again, but this time it said, "*if you do not you will die in these seats.*" CRAP! Now, I was shaken by what was said to me, but still it was not enough for me to let go of the bitterness that I held against my father.

Many years later, I was taking an inner healing class at my church called, *TheoPhostics*. It was facilitated by *Dr. Leeland Jones* and God was working on me... *showing 'me' ME!* One of the scriptures used was in *Ephesians 6:1-4*, **"Children obey your parents in the Lord for this is right. Honor thy father and thy mother, which is the first commandment with promise; That it may go well with thee, and thou mayest live long on the earth. And, ye fathers, provoke not your children to wrath: but bring them up in the nature and admonition of the Lord."**

I know that is a lot but let me help us today. First, is the point that God does not lie... He can't lie and He will not lie. The word of God is truth and Jesus is the Living Word and the bible is the written word or Truth. *Ephesians* shows us something wonderful in these verses; it says... "*Children obey your parents.*" But how? How do we obey our parents? "*In the Lord,*" because outside of the Lord, it is death and hardship and the only way to truly obey '*your parents*,' is in the perfected will of God. "*Honor thy father and thy mother*," honor means that no matter what happens, we as children must not speak against, disrespect or even challenge them. I know today's new age children have this thing about challenging what their parents say on every turn, that can constitute as dishonor. I began to think about what the Lord was saying here, '*to honor and not dishonor*.' After taking this course, the Lord began to soften my heart and I was able to, at least, speak about how I really felt, not just to show the face, that I put on in front of my family, friends and the Saints; you know when someone ask you how you doing, and you say, "*I'm blessed and highly favored*," but truth be told… *you are mad as all get out*.

It was a few years ago, while my wife and I was taking another course on inner healing called, *The Fathers Heart*, a good friend offered to pay for the course, because I wasn't going to take the course, but she said that the Lord told her to pay for the course because he wanted Lisa and I there. So, I went and this course was one of the weirdest classes I had ever taken in my life. The first thing they told us to do… was *to remove your religious hats and garments at the door; that we would not need them there*. People during the class, were allowed to pull chairs together and take a nap, if they wanted to just get downright comfortable. Now, by my coming from a disciplined formal church environment, this class was strange. The Lord began to move upon me during these 6 days and on the last day, the class was to write a letter to someone that hurt them. I began to write letters to my mother and then to my father; I asked them to forgive me for how I responded to who they were in my life. When I was adopted, I was asked by the Judge, '*if I wanted to change anything about my name*,' and he said, '*this was the time to do it*,' so I took the liberty at twelve years old to change my name completely. I wanted nothing to remind me of the people who left me and never came back; they cut me off and so, even from a twelve-year old's point of view, I had an opportunity to '*cut them off*' and '*out of my life*.'

As I was writing this letter, the Lord began to deal with me about *inheritance*. I was not understanding, but He kept saying inheritance; then I began to understand what my name meant. I saw what I did when I changed my name, (to spite my father… I was dishonoring him).

For many years, I would say that the song by the Temptations in 1972, *"Papa was a rolling stone where ever he laid his hat was his home, and when he die all he left us was alone."* He had children by several women and I was ashamed of him and did not want his name.

The Lord dealing with me, through writing that letter, broke something in me forever. I had completely forgiven my father and my mother many years prior to this class, but there was some residue left to bring to healing; *that was my name!* The Lord told me that by cutting my father off from my life, I actually cut myself off from the blessing that came with honoring my father. Wow! That blew my mind. I cut myself off from my blessing… *my inheritance.* The only inheritance that I knew of was abandonment, rejection, shame and hurt that is what I was rejecting; but by me dishonoring him the very thing I hated the most, I had become.

And not only that but the blessing that the bible said comes with honoring I negated. So that day in class, I decided to take my name back and when I wrote my name on the top of that paper it read, *Andrey Pernell Beecher,* that's who I am. Now, I have not legally changed back my name, but I no longer reject that name. I embrace who I am and honor my father and love my father.

I know there are many of you who may feel the same way. I felt and maybe you are not in the same situation that I came from, but you are going through right now and dealing with unforgiveness with your father or mother or have bitterness towards anyone. I offer you a way to freedom and that is through forgiveness. I said that my parents did not deserve forgiveness, but I was wrong. God tells us to honor father and mother, not because they are honorable but because He said so, this was not a request it was a command. If we honor, we will see the blessing, if we dishonor we will see the death that disobedience brings. Stop living in the shadows… **"Ye shalt also decree a thing, and it shall be established unto thee, and the light shall shine upon thy ways." Job 22:28. Come** into the marvelous light, *through forgiveness!*

This chapter will be talked about more in my upcoming book "Just Like My Father," which is about me not wanting to be like my dad, but because of my dishonoring him, I became him and how it almost cost me my marriage, THE THING I FEARED THE MOST HAS COME UPON ME" the release is coming soon.

NOTES

HOW DO YOU FEEL ABOUT THIS STORY

CHAPTER 32

—∞∞∞—

PRAYER FROM THE HEART

LORD JESUS, WE ASK YOU to identify with us as a little one being formed. Speak to him/her spirit and communicate with the little one that you knew about him/her and all the circumstances they entered into. You planned him/her Lord, and you delighted in his/her birth. Let him/her know that he/she is not a mistake, burden or an accident, *but a gift and a joy*.

Lord, I ask for your empowering to be able to forgive. By ourselves, we cannot forgive.

Lord, I ask you to remove the shame of *illegitimacy, abandonment and worthlessness*. You know what that feels like – they said you were illegitimate. Remove the shame of being born out of "*wedlock*." Lord, lift and minister to the hurt and anger of feeling unwelcomed, the fear that there will not be enough time, money or nurturing in not only my life, but in the lives of your people. Bring to death any confusion of gender – the secrecy, deception and isolation it causes. Lord, minister to the rejection of adoption, the betrayal of parental trust, the wound of having been lied to and stolen from.

Lord, wash MY heart clean of unconscious or hidden resentment. *Set me free*. Restore a sense of worth and purpose. Give me the gift of knowing that you have given me a special place in your family. Jesus, absorb any sense of futility. Communicate to my spirit your pride in me. Restore and draw forth my manliness, so that I may continue to be the man you made me to be. Grant me a boldness of *being* so that there is no fear in being seen. Lord, you create no mistakes! Write that deeply into my spirit. Pour your healing into the wounds caused from being teased or criticized. Let me cleave to your word, that "*Counsel is mine, and sound wisdom, I have understanding, I am strength.*" **(Proverbs 8:14)**

PRAYER FROM THE HEART

"*HE HAS A SECRET*"
Poem by Gerldine Wilson

He has a secret
He does not want to tell
If he felt like talking
He would say all is not well

His life is troubled...
It pains him so much
Because... the secret in his life is
He has been touched

Somebody's hands touched him
when he was at an early age
Defiled him all over and
filled him with rage

His manhood was questioned
when he was still just a boy
Instead of playing with blocks
he became someone's sex toy

Not touched by a stranger
It was somebody he knew
Trapped inside that touch
He didn't know what to do

He was left frightened
He was left confused
He was broken
because he was abused

Was he still a man?
He struggled in his mind
What happened to him in childhood
He could not leave behind

A boy became a man
But... all within him did not grow
Defilement of his spirit
helped to make it so
He had a secret
Some things he needed to say
Caught up in nightmares
That would not go away

Filled with the sounds
that overwhelmed his ears
reflections of pain
that still brought him to tears

He had a secret too big to maintain
A torturing on the inside too much to contain

Have you something hidden
Is it too big to be told
Has it made you feel cursed
Down to your very soul

Are you troubled by a touch
Is it too big to hold
Have the secrets in your life
gotten out of control?

God has the ability
Your every secret to hold

He knows the story
You have not yet told

He is not surprised
by anything you've gone through
Come tell your secret to him
who knows all about you

Look to the Father… Your Creator is He
He holds the power
to set all your secrets free!

THANK YOU

I would like to thank my wife Lisa for her support in writing this book. If it had not been for her this would have been a difficult step of Faith and that's what this was… a step of *"Faith."* My wife stood not only by me and supported me, but she was there *to pour into me* with sound wisdom. She reminded me that because of my propensity for frankness in relating experiences that "there is a thin line between *honesty* and indecent exposure." *My reference to honesty is not about revealing matters that should be sealed. Rather, it is my conviction that a man of God must be honest about who he is and what he was, and that his efforts in living the truth must line up with his faith confession. When a man of God is honest with himself, he is least likely to lie to others.*

I also want to thank my Senior Pastor, Bishop *Michael, and 1ˢᵗ Lady, Pastor Joyce Badger,* of *Bethesda World Harvest International Church* located at 1365 Main Street, Buffalo New York 14209, for their words of encouragement, in writing this book and the sound ministry that they have provided for myself, the congregation and the effective ministries that they have brought into the church, so that *the body of Christ* would grow spiritually, physically and emotionally.

I would like to *Dr. Leeland Jones,* Author of *Becoming Whole: Being the Beloved,* for his teachings in the area of inner healing and for being a tremendous source of information to propel my *inner healing.*

I would like to thank Sister *Angela Baker* for her interest in this book and taking it and proofing it for me, (she also has a book in print called *Just Like Joseph, published by Brentwood Christian Publishing,* "Check it out!").

I would like to thank, *Dr. Gloria Gibson,* for proofreading the first draft of this book and for giving me pointers on my content.

I would like to thank my Publisher, *iUniverse,* to SLB Academy, *Sheila Brown* and Editor, *Bernie Taylor.*

And, last but not least, to all of my *family, friends and supporters.* Thank you… *from my heart.*

Family: Erie County

Indicator(s) rate or percent (base year;current year)	Base Year Number	Base Year Rate	Current Year Number	Current Year Rate	NYS Current Rate
Foster Care Children In Care - Children/Youth 0-21 years, number and rate/1,000 children/youth ages birth-21 years (2010;2019) Data Sources | Narrative | Indicator Report	845	3.2	765	3.3	2.9
Child Abuse/Maltreatment - Indicated Reports of Child Abuse and Maltreatment, number and percent of reports (2010;2019) Data Sources | Narrative | Indicator Report	2,364	24.8	2,926	21.3	27.5
Foster Care TPR Judgments - Terminated Judgments, number and percent TPR determinations in given year (2010;2018) Data Sources | Narrative | Indicator Report	116	39.2	106	31.8	48.4
Foster Care TPR Judgments - Dismissed or Withdrawn Judgments, number and percent TPR determinations in given year (2010;2018) Data Sources | Narrative | Indicator Report	141	47.6	197	59.2	40.7
Foster Care TPR Judgments - Suspended Judgments, number and percent TPR determinations in given year (2010;2018) Data Sources | Narrative | Indicator Report	28	9.5	23	6.9	6.7
Foster Care TPR Judgments - Other Judgments, number and percent TPR determinations in given year (2010;2018) Data Sources | Narrative | Indicator Report	*11	*3.7	197	59.2	40.7
Foster Care Admissions - Children/Youth Admitted to Foster Care, number and rate/1,000 children/youth ages 0-21 years (2010;2019) Data Sources | Narrative | Indicator Report	431	2.0	496	2.1	1.5
Foster Care Discharges - Children/Youth Discharged from Foster Care, number and percent children/youth in foster care (2010;2019) Data Sources | Narrative | Indicator Report	497	37.0	554	42.0	35.8
Child Abuse/Maltreatment - Children/Youth in Indicated Reports of Abuse/Maltreatment, number and rate/1,000 children/youth ages 0-17 years (2010;2019) Data Sources | Narrative | Indicator Report	3,855	17.1	4,709	25.2	16.8
Foster Care Adoption Milestone - Children/Youth Freed for Adoption, number and percent children/youth in foster care (2010;2019) Data Sources | Narrative | Indicator Report	108	7.9	135	10.2	5.7
Foster Care Adoption Milestone - Children/Youth Discharged to Adoption, number and percent children/youth in foster care with goal and status of free for adoption (2010;2019) Data Sources | Narrative | Indicator Report	95	29.1	139	39.8	51.4

Created April 8, 2021 4:51 PM EST

NYSKWIC.org/get_data

The Adoption Option:

Children of all ages need permanent, stable, loving families. The Erie County Department of Social Services [ECDSS] is committed to ensuring that every child will know the love and caring of a permanent family.

Some children become available for adoption through the Department of Social Services when parents determine they are unable to care for their child/children and voluntarily surrender their child/children for adoption. Others become available when their parents are unable to make the necessary changes in their lives to keep their children safe. In those situations, Erie County Family Court may terminate parental rights of the child's parents, freeing the child for adoption. Children who are freed for adoption receive cash management services by caseworkers in adult and specialized services, sometimes in partnership with contract voluntary agencies. In addition to ongoing accountability to family court, caseworkers collaborate with services in mental health, juvenile justice, education, and other systems. Post adoptive services are arranged as needed.

When foster children become available for adoption, they are often adopted by their foster parent(s). Whenever possible, it is generally in a child's best interest for their first placement to be their last placement. Therefore, ECDSS makes a concerted effort to identify families to provide foster care who are also willing to consider adoption. Erie County also offers many kinds of supports to foster parents to help them as needs are identified during the placement.

Adoption Facts:

On average, there are approximately 300 children in Erie County awaiting adoption. Most have a family wanting to adopt them, but more than 50 children are still waiting to be adopted by their new family. These children range in age from 7-15 years old. Many have behavioral difficulties, the result of experiencing the instability of too many years in foster care without the security of a permanent family. Some have learning disabilities or physical disabilities.

There are services and supports to assist adoptive families in their care of these children. One can access and educate themselves to these resources by linking to http://www.ocfs.state.ny.us/adopt/post_adoption/.

To obtain the most up to date information about children available for adoption, visit: http://www.ocfs.state.ny.us/Adopt/

These are the children who most need a family to make a commitment to them, love them and guide them to a productive adulthood.

For more information, please call:
Resource Family Homefinding
@ [716] 658-7274

ERIE County
WWW2.ERIE.gov/socialservices.

135

GREAT FAMOUS PEOPLE
WHO ARE ADOPTED

Steve Jobs	Inventor, Micro Soft
Frances McDormand	Actress
Keegan Michael	Key Actor
John Lennon	Song Writer /Singer
Jammie Fox	Entertainer/ Actor
Dave Thomas	Wendy's Restaurant
Colin Kaepernick	Pro Football Player
Simone Biles	Olympic Gold Medalist
Maya Angelo	Prize Winning Poet
Babe Ruth Pro	Baseball Player
Eleanor Roosevelt	US President Theodor Roosevelt's Wife
Nelson Mandela	Nobel Peace Prize Winner and Former President of South Africa
Bill Clinton	US President
Gerald Ford	US President
Edger All Poe	American Writer known for his Poetry

So we are in great company- we are not alone. You can be what-ever you want, you can do what ever you set your heart and mind to do, the choice is up to you.

Scripture References Used In Book

Psalms 27:10 KJV

When my father and my mother forsake me, then the Lord will take me up.

Jeremiah 1:5a NKJV

Before I formed thee in the belly I knew thee; and before thou camest forth out of the womb I sanctified thee, and I ordained thee a prophet unto the nations.

Isaiah 49:14 – 16 NKJV

"Can a woman forget her nursing child,
[a]And not have compassion on the son of her womb?
Surely they may forget,
Yet I will not forget you.
16 See, I have inscribed you on the palms *of My hands;*
Your walls *are* continually before Me.

Philippians 4:13 NKJV

I can do all things through [a]Christ who strengthens me.

Romans 8:32 NKJV

And we know that all things work together for good to those who love God, to those who are the called according to *His* purpose.

John 12:15 NIV

And we know that all things work together for good to them that love God, to them who are the called according to his purpose.

Hebrew 12:15 KJV

looking carefully [a]lest *there be* any man that [b]falleth short of the grace of God; lest any root of bitterness springing up trouble *you*, and thereby the many be defiled;

Matthew 18:22 KJV

And when ye stand praying, forgive, if ye have ought against any: that your Father also which is in heaven may forgive you your trespasses.

John 2:15 KLV

And when he had made a scourge of small cords, he drove them all out of the temple, and the sheep, and the oxen; and poured out the changers' money, and overthrew the tables;

Ephesians 4:26 KJV

Be ye angry, and sin not: let not the sun go down upon your wrath:

Luke 6:28 KLV

Be ye angry, and sin not: let not the sun go down upon your wrath:

Luke 23:24 KLV

Then said Jesus, Father, forgive them; for they know not what they do. And they parted his raiment, and cast lots.

Genesis 4:13 NRSV

Then the LORD said to Cain, "Where is your brother Abel?" He said, "I do not know; am I my brother's keeper?"

Psalms 46:1-3 NRSV

od is our refuge and strength,
    a very present[a] help in trouble.
[2] Therefore we will not fear, though the earth should change,
    though the mountains shake in the heart of the sea;
[3] though its waters roar and foam,
    though the mountains tremble with its tumult. *Selah*

Proverbs 12:22 KJV

Lying lips are abomination to the LORD: but they that deal truly are his delight.

Matthew 6:14-16 NKJV

For if you forgive men their trespasses, your heavenly Father will also forgive you. [15] But if you do not forgive men their trespasses, neither will your Father forgive your trespasses.

John 8:36 KJV

For if you forgive men their trespasses, your heavenly Father will also forgive you. [15] But if you do not forgive men their trespasses, neither will your Father forgive your trespasses.

John 10:10 KJV

The thief cometh not, but for to steal, and to kill, and to destroy: I am come that they might have life, and that they might have it more abundantly.

Hebrews 12:6 NKJV

For whom the LORD loves He chastens,
And scourges every son whom He receives."

Hebrews 12:11 NKJV

No discipline is enjoyable while it is happening—it's painful! But afterward there will be a peaceful harvest of right living for those who are trained in this way.

John 15:5 KJV

I am the vine, ye are the branches: He that abideth in me, and I in him, the same bringeth forth much fruit: for without me ye can do nothing.

Jeremiah 29:11 NIV

For I know the plans I have for you," declares the LORD, "plans to prosper you and not to harm you, plans to give you hope and a future.

Hebrews 13:2 RSV

Do not neglect to show hospitality to strangers, for thereby some have entertained angels unawares.

Romans 12:19 NKJV

Beloved, do not avenge yourselves, but *rather* give place to wrath; for it is written, "Vengeance *is* Mine, I will repay," says the Lord.

Psalms 139:14 NKJV

I will praise You, for [a]I am fearfully *and* wonderfully made;
Marvelous are Your works,
And *that* my soul knows very well.

I Corinthians 10:13 KJV

There hath no temptation taken you but such as is common to man: but God is faithful, who will not suffer you to be tempted above that ye are able; but will with the temptation also make a way to escape, that ye may be able to bear it.

I Corinthians 4:15 WE

There hath no temptation taken you but such as is common to man: but God is faithful, who will not suffer you to be tempted above that ye are able; but will with the temptation also make a way to escape, that ye may be able to bear it.

Ephesians 1:4-6 KJV

There hath no temptation taken you but such as is common to man: but God is faithful, who will not suffer you to be tempted above that ye are able; but will with the temptation also make a way to escape, that ye may be able to bear it.

Matthew 1:18-25 KJV

Now the birth of Jesus Christ was as follows: After His mother Mary was betrothed to Joseph, before they came together, she was found with child of the Holy Spirit. [19]Then Joseph her husband, being [a]a just *man,* and not wanting to make her a public example, was minded to put her away secretly. [20]But while he thought about these things, behold, an angel of the Lord appeared to him in a dream, saying, "Joseph, son of David, do not be afraid to take to you Mary your wife, for that which is [b]conceived in her is of the Holy Spirit. [21]And she will bring forth a Son, and you shall call His name [c]Jesus, for He will save His people from their sins."

[22]So all this was done that it might be fulfilled which was spoken by the Lord through the prophet, saying: [23]"Behold, the virgin shall be with

child, and bear a Son, and they shall call His name Immanuel," which is translated, "God with us."

24 Then Joseph, being aroused from sleep, did as the angel of the Lord commanded him and took to him his wife,

Romans 8:15 NKJV

For you did not receive the spirit of bondage again to fear, but you received the Spirit of adoption by whom we cry out, "Abba,[a] Father."

Isaiah 53:3-6 KJV

He was despised and rejected by mankind,
    a man of suffering, and familiar with pain.
Like one from whom people hide their faces
    he was despised, and we held him in low esteem.
4 Surely he took up our pain
    and bore our suffering,
yet we considered him punished by God,
    stricken by him, and afflicted.
5 But he was pierced for our transgressions,
    he was crushed for our iniquities;
the punishment that brought us peace was on him,
    and by his wounds we are healed.
6 We all, like sheep, have gone astray,
    each of us has turned to our own way;
and the LORD has laid on him
    the iniquity of us all.

Hebrews 13:8 NIV

Jesus Christ is the same yesterday and today and forever.

Matthew 11:28-30 NIV

"Come to me, all you who are weary and burdened, and I will give you rest. ²⁹ Take my yoke upon you and learn from me, for I am gentle and humble in heart, and you will find rest for your souls. ³⁰ For my yoke is easy and my burden is light."

Romans 8:28-31 KJV

And we know that all things work together for good to them that love God, to them who are the called according to his purpose.

²⁹ For whom he did foreknow, he also did predestinate to be conformed to the image of his Son, that he might be the firstborn among many brethren.

³⁰ Moreover whom he did predestinate, them he also called: and whom he called, them he also justified: and whom he justified, them he also glorified.

³¹ What shall we then say to these things? If God be for us, who can be against us?

Romans 8:18 NAS

For I consider that the sufferings of this present time are not worthy *to be* compared with the glory that is to be revealed to us.

Joel 2:25 KJV

And I will restore to you the years that the locust hath eaten, the cankerworm, and the caterpillar, and the palmerworm, my great army which I sent among you.

II Thessalonians 3:16 KJV

Now the Lord of peace himself give you peace always by all means. The Lord be with you all.

Isaiah 10:27 KJV

And it shall come to pass in that day, that his burden shall be taken away from off thy shoulder, and his yoke from off thy neck, and the yoke shall be destroyed because of the anointing.

Isaiah 49:1-5 NIV

Listen to me, you islands;
    hear this, you distant nations:
Before I was born the LORD called me;

    from my mother's womb he has spoken my name.
² He made my mouth like a sharpened sword,
    in the shadow of his hand he hid me;
he made me into a polished arrow
    and concealed me in his quiver.
³ He said to me, "You are my servant,
    Israel, in whom I will display my splendor."

Romans 8:1 KJV

There is therefore now no condemnation to them which are in Christ Jesus, who walk not after the flesh, but after the Spirit.

John 3:16 KJV

For God so loved the world, that he gave his only begotten Son, that whosoever believeth in him should not perish, but have everlasting life.

Ephesians 6:1-4 KJV

Children, obey your parents in the Lord: for this is right.

[2] Honor thy father and mother; which is the first commandment with promise;

[3] That it may be well with thee, and thou mayest live long on the earth.

[4] And, ye fathers, provoke not your children to wrath: but bring them up in the nurture and admonition of the Lord.

Job 22:28 KJV

Children, obey your parents in the Lord: for this is right.

[2] Honor thy father and mother; which is the first commandment with promise;

[3] That it may be well with thee, and thou mayest live long on the earth.

[4] And, ye fathers, provoke not your children to wrath: but bring them up in the nurture and admonition of the Lord.

Proverbs 8:14 NKJV

Counsel is mine, and sound wisdom: I am understanding; I have strength.

Matthew 7:1-3 KJV

Judge not, that ye be not judged. For with what judgement, ye shall be judged: and with what measure ye mete, it shall be measured to you again. And why beholdest thou the mote that is in the brother's eye, but consider not the beam that is in thine own eye.

Ephesians 4:28 KLV

Philippians 4:19 KJV

But my God shall supply all your needs according to his riches in glory by Christ Jesus.

Exodus 23:26 KJV

There shall nothing cast their young, nor be barre, in thy land: the number of thy days I will fulfill.

Romans 12:19 ESV

Beloved, never avenge yourselves, but leave it to the wrath of God, for it is written, "vengeance is mine, I will repay, says the Lord."

I Timothy 6:10 NIV

For the love of money is a root of all kinds of evil Some people, eager for money, have wandered from the faith and pierced themselves with many griefs.

Isiah 54:17 NKJ

No weapon that is formed against thee shall prosper; and every tongue that shall rise against thee in judgement though shalt condemn. This is the heritage of the servants of the Lord, and their righteousness is of me, says the Lord.

Psalms 90:17 NIV

And the beauty of the Lord our God be upon us, And establish the work or our hands for us; Yes, establish the work of our hands.

Printed in the United States
by Baker & Taylor Publisher Services